The Go Programming Language

LANGUAGE

P H R A S E B O O K

David Chisnall

Addison-Wesley

DEVELOPER'S LIBRARY

Upper Saddle River, NJ · Boston · Indianapolis · San Francisco
New York · Toronto · Montreal · London · Munich · Paris · Madrid
Cape Town · Sydney · Tokyo · Singapore · Mexico City

Many of the designations used by manufacturers and sellers to distinguish their products are claimed as trademarks. Where those designations appear in this book, and the publisher was aware of a trademark claim, the designations have been printed with initial capital letters or in all capitals.

The author and publisher have taken care in the preparation of this book, but make no expressed or implied warranty of any kind and assume no responsibility for errors or omissions. No liability is assumed for incidental or consequential damages in connection with or arising out of the use of the information or programs contained herein.

The publisher offers excellent discounts on this book when ordered in quantity for bulk purchases or special sales, which may include electronic versions and/or custom covers and content particular to your business, training goals, marketing focus, and branding interests. For more information, please contact:

U.S. Corporate and Government Sales
(800) 382-3419
corpsales@pearsontechgroup.com

For sales outside the United States, please contact:

International Sales
international@pearson.com

Visit us on the Web: informit.com/aw

Library of Congress Cataloging-in-Publication Data:

Chisnall, David.
   The Go programming language phrasebook / David Chisnall.
      p. cm.
   Includes index.
   ISBN 978-0-321-81714-3 (pbk. : alk. paper) — ISBN 0-321-81714-1 (pbk. : alk. paper)
   1. Go (Computer program language) 2. Computer programming. 3. Open source software. I. Title.
   QA76.73.G63C45 2012
   005.3—dc23

                            2012000478

ISBN-13: 978- 0-321-81714-3
ISBN-10: 0-321-81714-1

Text printed in the United States on recycled paper at Edwards Brothers Malloy in Ann Arbor, Michigan.

First printing: March 2012

Editor-in-Chief Mark Taub	**Managing Editor** Kristy Hart	**Copy Editor** Gayle Johnson	**Cover Designer** Gary Adair
Acquisitions Editor Debra Williams Cauley	**Project Editor** Anne Goebel	**Publishing Coordinator** Andrea Bledsoe	**Senior Compositor** Gloria Schurick
Marketing Manager Stephane Nakib			

Table of Contents

About the Author

David Chisnall is a freelance writer and consultant. While studying for his PhD, he cofounded the Étoilé project, which aims to produce an open-source desktop environment on top of GNUstep, an open-source implementation of the OpenStep and Cocoa APIs. He is an active contributor to GNUstep and is the original author and maintainer of the GNUstep Objective-C 2 runtime library and the associated compiler support in the Clang compiler. He is also a FreeBSD committer working various aspects of the toolchain, including being responsible for the new C++ stack.

After completing his PhD, David hid in academia for a while, studying the history of programming languages. He finally escaped when he realized that there were places off campus with an equally good view of the sea and without the requirement to complete quite so much paperwork. He occasionally returns to collaborate on projects involving modeling the semantics of dynamic languages.

When not writing or programming, David enjoys dancing Argentine tango and Cuban salsa, playing badminton and ultimate frisbee, and cooking.

Acknowledgments

The first person I'd like to thank is Mark Summerfield, author of *Programming in Go: Creating Applications for the 21st Century*. If you finish this book and want to learn more, I'd recommend you pick up a copy. Mark was the person responsible for making me look at Go in the first place.

The next person I need to thank is Yoshiki Shibata. Yoshiki has been working on the Japanese translation of this book and, in doing so, has sent me countless emails highlighting areas that could be improved. If you enjoy reading this book then Yoshiki deserves a lot of the credit.

Finally, I need to thank everyone else who was involved in bringing this book from my text editor to your hands. A lot of people have earned some credit along the way. In particular, Debra Williams-Cauley, who masterminded the project, and Anne Goebel, who shepherded the book from a draft manuscript to the version you now hold.

Introducing Go

When learning a new language, there are three
things that you need to understand. The first
and most important is the abstract model that
the language presents. The next is the concrete
syntax. Finally, you need to learn your way
around the standard libraries and the common
idioms of the language.

This chapter will look at the abstract model
that Go presents to programmers. If you want
to dive straight into real examples, skip to the
next chapter, which covers the concrete syntax.
The rest of the book will cover highlights from
the Go standard library and the various idioms
that you will find common in Go code.

Go and C

In the late '60s, a small team at the Bell Telephone
Laboratories wrote a simple operating system
called UNICS, a very lightweight system inspired

by the MULTICS project, on the PDP-7 minicomputer that they had access to. When they wanted to port it to another system, they had to rewrite all of the code, which was written in PDP-7 assembly language.

To make the transition easier, they wanted to be able to share as much code as possible between different versions. They needed a language that was sufficiently low-level that a simple compiler (the only kind that existed in the '60s) could generate efficient machine code from it, yet which hid most of the irrelevant details of the target machine. BCPL was close, but it was too complex in some areas and lacked some required features in others.

Dennis Ritchie created the C programming language as a derivative of BCPL, and eventually most of the PDP-11 version of UNIX was rewritten in it. When UNIX was ported to the VAX, they just needed to retarget the compiler and write a small amount of very low-level assembly code. The majority of the system could be recompiled without modification.

Since its initial public release in 1978, C has become a very popular language. It is the de facto standard low-level language for programming these days, and it even finds use in a significant amount of application development.

The point of a low-level language is to provide an abstract machine model to the programmer that closely reflects the architecture of the concrete machines that it will target. There is no such thing as a universal low-level language: a language that closely represents the architecture of a PDP-11 will not accurately reflect something like a modern GPU or even an old B5000 mainframe. The attraction of C has been that, in providing an abstract model similar to a PDP-11, it is similar to most cheap consumer CPUs.

Over the last decade, this abstraction has become less like the real hardware. The C abstract model represents a single processor and a single block of memory. These days, even mobile phones have multicore processors, and a programming language designed for single-processor systems requires significant effort to use effectively. It is increasingly hard for a compiler to generate machine code from C sources that efficiently uses the resources of the target system.

In 2007, Robert Griesemer, Pike, and Ken Thompson began work on a new language. Thompson had both been instrumental in the creation of C and Pike had worked on it later at Bell Labs, being members of the original UNIX team that drove the development of C. The aim of Go, their new language, was to fill the same niche today that C fit into in the '80s. It is a low-level language for multiprocessor development. Experience with C taught them that a successful systems programming language ends up being used for application development, so Go incorporates a number of high-level features, allowing developers to use it for things like web services or desktop applications, as well as very low-level systems.

Both Pike and Thompson worked on Plan 9[1], a system designed to be a "better UNIX than UNIX." Plan 9 eventually gave birth to the Inferno distributed operating system. For Inferno, Pike created the Limbo programming language. If you've used Limbo, you will find a lot of ideas very similar. The module system, channel-based communication, garbage collection, much of the type system, and even a lot of the syntax in Go are inherited directly from Limbo. The reference implementation of Go is based on the Plan 9 compiler toolchain.

If you come from C, then many things in Go will seem familiar, but some will seem strange. As a trivial example, variable declarations in Go usually look like they are written back to front to C programmers, although if you come from other members of the Algol family, such as Pascal, then these may not seem so strange. Most of these changes come from decades of experience working with C, and seeing ways in which it can be improved.

Why Go?

In recent years, scalability has become a lot more important than raw speed. Moore's law tells us

---

[1]Named after the film *Plan 9 from Outer Space.*

that the number of transistors on a CPU can
be expected to double roughly every 18 months.
For a long time, this roughly corresponded to a
doubling in performance for a single thread of
execution. Now, it generally means that you get
twice as many cores.

It used to be that you just had to wait six
months, and your C code would run twice as
fast on a new machine. This is no longer true.
Now, if you want your code to be faster on new
machines, then it must be parallel.

C is inherently a serial language. Various
libraries, such as POSIX threads and OpenMP,
make it possible to write multithreaded code in
C, but it's very hard to write code that scales
well. In creating DragonFly BSD, Matt Dillon
observed that there was no point in creating
an N:M threading model—where N userspace
threads are multiplexed on top of M kernel
threads—because C code that uses more than a
handful of threads is very rare.

Go, in contrast, was designed with concurrency
in mind. If you write idiomatic Go, then you
will write code that, conceptually, does lots of
things in parallel. The compiler and runtime
environment can easily run this code on a single
core by simply timeslicing between the various
parts. They can also run it on a manycore
machine by distributing the tasks across different
threads.

This is a very important advantage. In the

past, I had to write some code that would work on my single-core laptop and yet scale up to a 64-processor SGI machine. Doing this in C was very hard, but doing the same thing in Erlang was trivial. In Erlang, I wrote code that used over a thousand Erlang processes, and the runtime automatically distributed them across the available cores.

The disadvantage of the Erlang version was that Erlang performs significantly worse than C in a single thread. Until you have a large number of available cores, the single-threaded C version will be faster than the concurrent Erlang version.

Go combines the best of both worlds. In single-threaded performance, it is close to C, yet it encourages a programming style that scales well to large numbers of cores. It's important to remember that the number of available cores is likely to follow a geometric growth pattern. Currently, two to eight cores is common[2] and machines with more than about 16 cores are expensive. In a few years, you will see mobile phones with 64 cores and laptops with even more. Writing C code that scales to two, or even eight cores is quite difficult but not insanely hard. Writing C code that scales to 64 or 256 cores is very challenging. With a language designed for concurrency, it is much easier.

Concurrency is the most obvious advantage

---

[2]If you are reading this book in a few years, this will probably seem laughably dated.

of Go, but it is not the only one. Go aims to
provide a rich set of features without overcomplicating
the language. Contrast this with C++, where
even after having worked on a standard library
implementation and a couple of compilers for the
language, I still find myself having to refer to the
spec periodically.

Go also includes a rich standard library, which
makes developing complex web applications easy.
It provides a number of mid-level abstractions,
which provide high-level access to low-level
features. We'll look at one of those in detail in
Chapter 5, *Arrays and Slices*.

Goroutines and Channels

The fundamental concurrency primitive in Go
is the *goroutine*. This is a pun on coroutine, a
method of flow control popularized by Simula. A
goroutine is a like function call that completes
asynchronously. Conceptually, it runs in parallel,
but the language does not define how this
actually works in terms of real parallelism.

A Go compiler may spawn a new operating
system thread for every goroutine, or it may
use a single thread and use timer signals to
switch between them. The exact implementation
mechanism for goroutines is not specified by the
language and may change over time.

By themselves, goroutines are not very useful.
C lets you create threads almost as easily as

Go lets you create goroutines, yet that doesn't make it easy to write concurrent code in C. Creating concurrent subprograms (threads, child processes, or goroutines) is the easy part of the problem. The difficult part is communicating between them.

C does not provide any primitives for communicating between threads, because C does not recognize threads; they are implemented in libraries. Threads all share an address space, so it is possible to write your own code for communicating between them, and anyone who has written concurrent C code has probably done this at least once.

Go, in contrast, is designed for concurrency. It uses a form of C. A. R. Hoare's *Communicating Sequential Processes (CSP)* formalism to facilitate communication between goroutines. CSP defines communication channels that events can be sent down. Go programs can create channels and use them to communicate between threads.

A good rule of thumb for concurrent code is that the complexity of debugging it is proportional to the number of concurrent tasks multiplied by the number of possible ways in which they can interact. Because C threads use a shared-everything model, the number of possible ways in which they can interact is very large.

This is made worse by the fact that it is trivial for errors in code using pointers to mean that two C threads are sharing a data structure that

they shouldn't, for example via a buffer overrun
or a dangling pointer. These problems do not
manifest in Go because Go adds one feature
to C and removes another. Go programs use
garbage collection, making dangling pointers
impossible, and disallows pointer arithmetic,[3]
making most other categories of pointer-related
errors impossible. We'll look at this later, in
Understanding the Memory Model.

Creating a goroutine is intended to be much
cheaper than creating a thread using a typical C
threading library. The main reason for this is the
use of *segmented stacks* in Go implementations.

The memory model used by early C implementations
was very simple. Code was mapped (or copied)
into the bottom of the address space. Heap
(dynamic memory) space was put in just above
the top of the program, and the stack grew down
from the top of the address space. Low-level
memory management worked using the `brk()`
system call to add more pages at the top of the
heap segment and the `sbrk()` call to add more
pages at the bottom of the stack segment.

Threading complicated this. The traditional C
stack was expected to be a contiguous block of
memory. When you create a new thread, you
need to allocate a chunk of memory big enough
for the maximum stack size. Typically, that's
about 1MB of RAM. This means that creating
a thread requires allocating 1MB of RAM, even

---

[3]Except via the unsafe package.

if the thread is only ever going to use a few KB of stack space. This is required because compiled C code assumes that it can allocate more stack memory by moving the stack pointer. Operating systems usually mark the page below the bottom of the stack as no-access, so small stack overflows will cause a segmentation fault.

Go functions are more clever. They treat the stack as a linked list of memory allocations. If there is enough space in the current stack page for their use, then they work like C functions; otherwise they will request that the stack grows. A short-lived goroutine will not use more than the 4KB initial stack allocation, so you can create a lot of them without exhausting your address space, even on a 32-bit platform.

Goroutines are not intended to be implemented as kernel threads. The language does not make hard guarantees on their concurrency. Like Java threads or Erlang processes, a large number of goroutines can be multiplexed onto a small number of kernel threads. This means that context switches between goroutines is often cheaper than between POSIX threads.

Selecting a Compiler

At the time of writing, there are two stable Go compilers. The reference implementation is Gc, although it is commonly referred to as *6g*. This is based on the Plan 9 compiler toolchain.

The Plan 9 toolchain programs are named with a number indicating the architecture that they target, followed by a letter indicating their function. The three architectures supported by Go are ARM (5), x86-64 (6), and i386 (8). If you are using ARM, you would use the 5g command instead of 6g to compile Go programs, and 5l instead of 6l to link them.

The alternative is a front end for the *GNU Compiler Collection (GCC)*, called gccgo. This turns Go code into more or less the same intermediate representation that GCC uses for Fortran, C, and C++, and then subjects it to the same set of optimizations, again producing native code.

Currently, Gc is probably the better choice, although gccgo is starting to produce better code. It is the reference implementation of Go, and so is the subject of the most active development. There are several important differences between them, however.

The most obvious is that gccgo uses operating system threads to implement goroutines, and will not use segmented stacks in all configurations. This means that creating a goroutine is as expensive as creating a thread in C. If you are writing code with a high order of parallelism, then this will make gccgo much slower than 6g. If your code only uses a few goroutines, and doesn't create them very frequently, then the better optimization back end in GCC may make it faster.

It's worth remembering that both compilers produce native executables. Go uses the same implementation model as Objective-C: native binaries and a small runtime library implementing the dynamic functionality. There is no virtual machine interpreting or JIT-compiling code. It would be possible to write a dynamic recompilation environment for Go, but the current implementations are static compilers. This means that distributing an application written in Go is as easy as distributing an application written in any other compiled language. You need to include any libraries that you use, but users don't need a large runtime environment, as they do with .NET, Java, or Python code, for example.

Since Go is a relatively new language, there will almost certainly be new implementations appearing over time. For example, it is currently possible to use the gcc front end with the LLVM code generator via the DragonEgg plugin, and a native Go front end for LLVM is likely to appear at some point.

Creating a Simple Go Program

```
0   $ 6g hello.go
1   $ 6l hello.6
2   $ ./6.out
3   Hello World!
4   $ go run hello.go
5   Hello World!
```

If you're using the Gc compiler, then you need to invoke the version of it specific to your architecture. If you're on an x86-64 system, then this will be 6g. This takes a list of Go source files and produces object code. The object code must then be linked to produce the final binary.

At first glance, this is very similar to C, where you also first run the compiler and then the linker. There are a number of differences, which mostly make Go easier to compile.

When you run 6g, it looks for **import** directives and inserts references to the relevant packages into the object code. This means that you usually don't need to specify any libraries to the linker: it will read the required packages from the object code file that you give it and link all of those into the resulting executable.

The linking step is needed to combine all of the Go packages that you use, along with any C libraries that you call via the foreign function interface, into a single executable. The compiler performs partial linking to produce packages.

The final linking step is only required when you want to import all of the separate bits of code and combine them with the system-specific preamble that all executables share.

The compiler and linker both generate default filenames from the target architecture. In the example at the start of this section, the 6g compiler generates a hello.6 object code file. If you used 8g instead, and generated 32-bit x86 code, then the resulting file would be hello.8 and the 8l linker would produce 8.out instead of 6.out. These are just the default output filenames. You can use -o with both tools to specify another filename.

As of Go 1.0, all of the details of this are typically hidden from you. The go command can compile and run programs for you with a single step. Simply type go run followed by the name of the source file and it will do all of this for you. If you specify the -x flag, then you can see exactly what this tool does as it runs.

The Go Type System

Go is a language with static typing and tight coupling between components. Go is also a language with dynamic typing and loose coupling between components. The language allows you to select which of these is more appropriate for each use case.

Go has a range of C-like primitive types and

structures that are similar to C structures, with the addition of methods (which are allowed on all Go types, not just structures) but without any form of inheritance. If you call a method on an expression with a static type directly, then the methods on it are just syntactic sugar on function calls. They are statically looked up and called.

The other side of the Go type system is visible via interfaces. Unlike Java interfaces or Objective-C protocols, they support *duck typing*[4] and don't have to be explicitly adopted. Any type that implements the methods that an interface lists implicitly implements that interface. If you've used languages in the Smalltalk family, including Python or Ruby, then you're probably familiar with duck typing.

Interface types can be used as variable types. When you call any method on an interface-typed variable, it uses dynamic dispatch to find the correct method implementation.

Go also supports *introspection* on types. You can query any variable to find out whether it is an instance of a specified type, or whether it implements a specified interface. This makes it easy to write generic data structures in Go. You can either define an interface specifying the methods that you require, or use the *empty interface*, which can be used to represent any

---

[4]If it walks like a duck and quacks like a duck, it's a duck.

type (including primitive types) if you are just storing values and don't need to call any methods.

One of the most useful features for a lazy programmer is the *type inference* that the Go compiler does. This allows you to avoid explicit type annotations on most variable declarations. If you combine initialization with declaration, then the compiler will infer the variable's type from the type of the expression assigned to it.

Understanding the Memory Model

Go uses *garbage collection (GC)*. Generally, people have one of two reactions to this. If you come from a high-level language, like Java, C#, Ruby, Python, or Smalltalk, then your reaction is likely to be "So what? It's a standard language feature these days." People coming from C or C++, in contrast, tend to regard GC as a decadent luxury and a sign of incompetence among programmers in general. Oh, and they also want you to get off their lawn.

Garbage collection means that you don't have to think about when to deallocate memory. In Go, you explicitly allocate values, but they are automatically reclaimed when they are no longer required. There is no equivalent of C's **free()** or C++'s **delete**. As with other garbage collected languages, it is still possible to leak objects if you accidentally keep references to them after you stop using them.

When you're writing single-threaded code, garbage collection is a luxury. It's nice to have, but it's not a vital feature. This changes when you start writing multithreaded code. If you are sharing pointers to an object between multiple threads, then working out exactly when you can destroy the object is incredibly hard. Even implementing something like reference counting is hard. Acquiring a reference in a thread requires an atomic increment operation, and you have to be very careful that objects aren't prematurely deallocated by race conditions.

Like Java, and unlike C or C++, Go does not explicitly differentiate between stack and heap allocations. Memory is just memory. If you create an object with local scope, then current implementations will allocate it on the stack unless it has its address taken somewhere. Future implementations might always allocate it in a young GC generation and then move it to another generation if it has remaining references after a short amount of time. Alternatively, they may perform better escape analysis to allocate objects on the stack even if they have their address taken, as long as they are never referenced after the function in which they are allocated returns.

Go is designed to make garbage collection relatively easy to implement, although the

existence of interior pointers makes it harder
than a language like Java or Smalltalk. There
are strict restrictions on where pointers can
be stored, so the collector can, in theory,
always tell, for example, the difference between
an integer and a pointer value. In current
implementations, Go uses fairly conservative
garbage collection, although that is one of the
areas that is likely to improve in future versions.

Because Go is designed for concurrency, the
memory model defines explicitly what to expect
when two goroutines touch the same memory:
in short, there are no guarantees. Go does
not enforce any constraints on the order that
memory accesses occur with regard to each
other. The compiler is free to reorder any
memory accesses within a goroutine, as long as
that reordering does not alter the semantics of
the goroutine running in isolation. For example,
consider the following bit of pseudocode:

```
a = b;
use(b)
use(a);
b = 12;
```

The compiler is free to rearrange the statements
so that the user-visible effect is not changed
within the scope of this block. For example, this
would be a valid reordering:

```
use(b)
a = b;
b = 12;
```

```
use(a);
```

Although the statements reading and writing
the values of the two variables are no longer in
the same order, it is not possible for the user
to distinguish the difference. This means that
you have to be very careful when using shared
memory from two goroutines: if either variable
in this example is shared then this kind of
optimization would have confusing consequences.
In general, it's a good idea to only share read-
only strutures. We'll look at some alternatives
for mutable data in Chapter 10, *Concurrency
Design Patterns*.

A Go Primer

One of the goals of Go was a consistent and unambiguous syntax. This makes it easy for tools to examine Go programs, and also makes it easy to learn. Unhelpful compiler errors make it difficult to learn a language, as anyone who has made a typo in C++ code using templates will know.

In C, for example, function and global variable declarations have almost the same syntax. This means that the compiler can't easily tell which one you meant if you make an error. It gives you helpful error messages like "expected ;" on a line where you don't think a semicolon is expected at all.

The Go grammar was designed to make it possible for the compiler to tell you more accurately what you did wrong. It was also designed to avoid the need to state something that can be easily inferred. For example, if you create a variable and set its value to 42, the compiler could probably guess that this variable should be an integer, without it being explicitly stated. If you initialize it with a function call, then the compiler can definitely tell that the type should be whatever the function returned. This was the same problem that C++ 2011 solves with the **auto** type.

Go adopts JavaScript's idea of *semicolon insertion*, and takes it a step further. Any line that can be interpreted as a complete statement has a semicolon implicitly inserted at the end by the parser.[1] This means that Go programs can freely omit semicolons as statement terminators. This adds some constraints, for example enforcing a brace style where open braces are at the end of the line at the start of flow-control statements, rather than on their own. If you happen to be a human, this is unfortunate, because it means that you can't use the highly optimized symmetry recognition paths, which evolution has spent the last million or so years optimizing in your visual cortex, for recognizing code blocks.

This chapter contains an overview of Go syntax. This is not a complete reference. Some aspects are covered in later chapters. In particular, all of the concurrency-related aspects of Go are covered in Chapter 9, *Goroutines*.

---

[1] This is an oversimplification. The exact rules for semicolon insertion are more complicated, but this rule of thumb works in most cases.

The Structure of a Go Source File

```go
package main
import "fmt"

func main() {
  fmt.Printf("Hello World!\n")
}
```

From: hello.go

A Go source file consists of three parts. The first is a **package** statement. Go code is arranged in packages, which fill the rôles of both libraries and header files in C. The package in this example is called **main**, which is special. Every program must contain a **main** package, which contains a **main()** function, which is the program entry point.

The next section specifies the packages that this file uses and how they should be imported. In this example, we're importing the **fmt** package.

Once the **fmt** package has been imported, any of its exported types, variables, constants, and functions can be used, prefixed by the name of the package. In this simple example, we're calling **Printf()**, a function similar to C's **printf**, to print "Hello World!" in the terminal.

Although Go uses static compilation, it's important to realize that **import** statements are much closer to Java or Python import

directives than to C inclusions. They do not
include source code in the current compilation
unit. Unlike Java and Python packages, Go
packages are imported when the code is linked,
rather than when it is run. This ensures that a
Go application will not fail because of a missing
package on the deployment system, at the cost
of increasing the size of the executable. Packages
in Go are more important than in languages like
Java, because Go only provides access control at
the package level, while Java provides it at the
class level.

When you compile a package (from one or
more .go files) with the Gc compiler, you get an
object code file for the package. This includes
a metadata section that describes the types
and functions that the package exports. It also
contains a list of the packages that this package
imports.

The input to the 6l linker is always a .6 file for
the main package. This file contains references
to every package that the main package imports,
which may in turn reference further packages.
The linker then combines them all.

This eliminates one of the most irritating
problems with building complex C programs:
you include a header, and then have to work out
which library provided it and add the relevant
linker flags. With Go, if a package compiles, it
will link. You don't have to provide any extra
flags to the linker to tell it to link things that

you've referenced via **import** directives.

The remainder of a Go file contains declarations of types, variables, and functions. We'll explore that for the rest of this chapter.

You may find that you have two packages that you want to import that have the same name. This would cause problems in Go. The badStyleImport.go example is functionally equivalent to the example at the start of this section but renames the **fmt** package, calling it **format**. Renaming a package when you import it is usually a bad idea, because it makes your code harder for people to read. You should only ever use it when you explicitly need to disambiguate two packages with the same name.

```
0  package main
1  import format "fmt"
2
3  func main() {
4    format.Printf("Hello World!\n")
5  }
```

From: badStyleImport.go

Declaring Variables

```
4    var i int
5    var θ float32
6    var explicitly, typed, pointers *complex128
7    int_pointer := &i
8    another_int_pointer := new(int)
9    generic_channel := make(chan interface{})
```

From: variables.go

Variables are declared with the **var** keyword,
followed by the variable name, and finally
by the type. The existence of a specific
keyword for variable declarations makes it
easy to differentiate them from other types of
statements.

Writing the type at the end looks weird to
people familiar with C-family languages, but it
makes sense when you read the code. A (typed)
variable declaration is an instruction saying, for
example, "declare the variable foo to have the
type int."

One of the variables declared at the start of this
section uses θ (theta) as a variable name. Go
permits identifiers to start with any symbols that
Unicode classes as letters. This can sometimes
be very useful, such as if variable names are
mathematical quantities. Don't abuse it, though:
the person maintaining your code will not thank
you if you use characters that he can't type on
his keyboard for frequently used variables.

A declaration statement may declare multiple

variables, but they all have the same type. In C, some may have the type that is written at the start of the declaration, some may be pointers to that type, some may be pointers to pointers to that type, and so on. The form used by Go is far less prone to ambiguity.

You will rarely use the long form of declarations. One of the key ideas in writing good code is the *principle of minimum scope*. This means that the scope of a variable—the lexical region where it is valid—should be as small as possible for the variable's lifetime. One corollary of this is that variables should be declared immediately before their first use and initialized as part of their declaration.

Go provides a shorthand syntax, the `:=` initialization operator, which does this. Using this notation, you can declare and initialize a variable in a single statement. More importantly, you avoid the need to declare a type for the variable: the type of the variable is the type of the expression used to initialize it.

The example at the start of this section shows both kinds of declaration. It also introduces Go's syntax for pointers. The variable `int_pointer` is initialized using the *address-of operator (&)*. This should be familiar to C programmers: it returns the address in memory of an object. The returned value, however, is more similar to a Java reference than a C pointer. You can't perform arithmetic using Go pointers,

nor use them interchangeably with arrays. As
with Java references, you can pass Go pointers
around without having to worry about when
the underlying object will be deallocated. It will
automatically be freed when the last reference is
destroyed. Unlike Java references, you can make
pointers to primitive types, not just to structures
(Go's equivalent of objects).

In this example, you could return `int_pointer`
from this function without any problems. This
may seem strange to C programmers, because
it points to a variable declared locally. The Go
compiler will try to allocate `i` on the stack,
but that's just an implementation detail. If its
address is taken and it is returned from the
function then it will be allocated on the heap
instead.

This example creates another integer pointer,
in a different way. The `new()` built-in function
creates a new integer and returns a pointer to
it. This is semantically equivalent to declaring
an integer variable and then taking its address.
Neither guarantees how the underlying storage
will be allocated. You can pass any type
to `new()`, but it is not the standard way of
allocating everything.

Go includes three special types, which we'll
look at in a lot more detail later in this book:
slices, *maps*, and *channels*. These are *reference
types*, meaning that you always access them via
a reference. If you assign one map-typed variable

to another, then you will have two variables referring to the same map. In contrast, if you assign one integer-typed variable to another, then you will have two variables with the same value, but modifying one will not affect the other.

Instances of reference types in Go are created with the make() built-in function. This is similar to new(), but also performs initialization of the built-in types. Values returned by new() are simply zeroed. They are not guaranteed to be immediately useful, although good style suggests that they should be.

Declaring Functions

```go
func printf(str string, args ...interface{}) (int
    , error) {
    _, err := fmt.Printf(str, args...)
    return len(args), err
}

func main() {
    count := 1
    closure := func(msg string) {
        printf("%d %s\n", count, msg)
        count++
    }
    closure("A Message")
    closure("Another Message")
}
```

From: functions.go

Functions in Go are declared using the **func** keyword. As with variable declarations, the return type goes at the end. This can be a single value, or a list of values. The printf() function in the example shows several important features of Go. This is a *variadic function*, which returns multiple values: an integer and an error. The integer is the number of variadic arguments passed to it, and the error code is one of the values returned from the Printf() function from the *fmt package*.

Note the syntax for calling functions that return multiple values. The return values must either all be ignored, or all assigned to variables. The *blank identifier*, _, can be used for values that you wish to discard.

Variadic functions in Go are particularly interesting. In C, a variadic function call just pushes extra parameters onto the stack, and the callee has to know how to pop them off. In Go, all variadic parameters are delivered as a *slice* (see Chapter 5, *Arrays and Slices*; for now you can think of a slice as being like an array). The variadic parameters must all be of the same type, although you can use the *empty interface type* (**interface{}**) to allow variables of any type and then use type introspection to find out what they really are.

The main() function in the example is the program entry point. Unlike many other languages, this takes no arguments. Command-line arguments and environment variables are stored globally in Go, making it easy to access them from any function, not just one near the program entry point.

Inside this function, you'll see a closure defined. Closures in Go are declared as anonymous functions, inside other functions. The closure can refer to any variables in the scope where it is declared. In this example, it refers to the `count` variable from the outer function's scope. It would continue to do so even after the outer function returned. In Go, there is no distinction between heap and stack allocated variables, except at the implementation level. If a local variable is referenced after the function that contains it, then it is not freed when the function returns. If `closure` were stored in a global variable, for example, then `count` would not be deallocated, even after the function returned.

Looping in Go

```go
package main
import "fmt"

func main() {
  loops := 1
  // while loop:
  for loops > 0 {
    fmt.Printf("\nNumber of loops?\n")
    fmt.Scanf("%d", &loops)
    // for loop
    for i := 0 ; i < loops ; i++ {
      fmt.Printf("%d ", i)
    }
  }
  // Infinite loop
  for {
    // Explicitly terminated
    break
  }
}
```

From: loop.go

In C, you have three kinds of loops, all with different syntax and overlapping semantics. Go manages to have more expressive loop semantics, but simple and uniform syntax.

Every loop in Go is a **for** statement. We'll only look at the forms that mirror C loop constructs here. The form that iterates over a collection is explained in Chapter 5, *Arrays and Slices*.

The loop.go example shows the three types of general **for** loops in Go. The last one is the simplest. This is an infinite loop, with an explicit **break** statement to terminate it. You'd most commonly use this form for an event loop that would not terminate in normal use. Like C, Go also has a **continue** statement that immediately jumps to the start of the next loop iteration, or exits the loop if the loop condition no longer holds.

Both the **break** and **continue** statements support an optional label for jumping out of nested loops. Note that the label is not a jump target; it is just used to identify the loop.

```
5    for i := 0 ; i<10 ; i++ {
6  L:
7      for {
8        for {
9          break L
10         }
11       }
12       fmt.Printf("%d\n", i)
13     }
```

From: break.go

You can see this in the break.go example. The **break** statement jumps out of the two inner loops, but does not prevent the Printf call from running. It jumps to the end of the loop immediately after L:, not to the start.

Most of the time, you won't use infinite loops and explicit escapes. The other two types of **for** loops in Go are analogous to `while` and **for** loops in C and the older form of **for** loops in

Java. The outer loop in the example at the start of this section will test its condition and loop as long as it is true. The inner loop first performs the initialization (i := 0) then tests the loop condition (i < loops), and runs the loop clause as long as it's true. Between each loop iteration, it runs the increment clause (i++). If you've used any vaguely C-like language, then this will be very familiar to you. The only difference between a Go **for** loop and a C **for** loop is that the Go version does not require brackets.

There are a couple of interesting things in this loop. The first is the creation of the loop variable (i) at the loop scope. This is similar to C99 or C++. The variable that is declared in the loop initialization clause is only in scope for the duration of the loop.

The second is the *increment statement.* Note that I did not call it a *postincrement expression.* The designers of Go decided to eliminate the confusion between preincrement and postincrement expressions in C. In Go, the increment statement is not an expression, and only the suffix syntax is allowed. This line increments the variable, but it does not evaluate to anything. Writing something like a := b++ is not valid Go. Writing ++b is invalid in all contexts in Go: there is no prefix form of the operator.

Creating Enumerations

```go
const (
    Red                = (1<<iota)
    Green              = (1<<iota)
    Blue, ColorMask    = (1<<iota), (1<<(iota+1))-1
)
```

From: enum.go

There are several places in Go where it is obvious that someone has spent a lot of thought designing exactly the right syntax for most common uses of a language feature. Enumeration constants are the most obvious example of this attention to detail.

There is no divide between constants and enumerations in Go. This mirrors their implementation in C, where enumerated types can be used interchangeably with integers. Groups of constants within the same declaration in Go are used for enumerations.

There are two common uses for enumerated types. The first is defining a set of mutually-exclusive options. The second is defining a set of overlapping flags. Typically, you'll use a sequence of numbers for the first and a sequence of powers of 2 for the second. You can then create a bitfield by bitwise-oring a combination of enumeration values together.

In C, and most other languages with enumerated types, you need to explicitly provide the numerical values for the second type of enumeration. The first will be automatically numbered by the compiler.

Go provides a much more flexible mechanism for defining enumerations. The `iota` predeclared identifier is similar to the GNU C `__COUNTER__` preprocessor macro, but it's more powerful. It is an integer constant expression. In a normal program scope, it evaluates to zero, but in the scope of a constant declaration it is initially zero but then incremented on each line where it is used.

Unlike `__COUNTER__`, `iota` is scoped. It is zero on the first line of the group in this example, and will always be zero in the first line of this group, irrespective of how it is used elsewhere. If you have multiple **const** groups in a single source file, then `iota` will be zero at the start of each of them.

The example at the start of this section shows how to declare a group of constants for use as an enumerated type. This simple example shows the low 3 bits of a bitfield being used to store three flags indicating the presence of three color values. The `ColorMask` constant is defined to provide the value that must be bitwise-and'd with an integer to give the three color flags.

It's possible to reference constants from other constant declarations, so you can combine this kind of declaration easily. For example, you could provide another constant declaration

describing another group of flags within a set,
and then extend this declaration to use them in
the next few bits of the bitfield.

Similarly, you can extend existing constant
declarations by inserting another **iota** expression
earlier. This will then renumber all subsequent
values, so it's important to be careful when the
constants are part of a binary interface.

Constants—and therefore enumerations—in
Go are not limited to integers. Other types
can be specified in the same way. The **enum.go**
example also shows the declaration of the
complex constant **i**, with the same definition as
in mathematics.

```
10  const (
11    i complex128 = complex(0, 1)
12  )
```

From: enum.go

Declaring Structures

```
4  type Example struct {
5    Val string
6    count int
7  }
```

From: struct.go

Structures in Go are somewhat richer than

C structures. One of the most important
differences is that Go structures automatically
support *data hiding*.

Any top-level type, method, or variable name
that starts with a capital letter is visible outside
of the package in which it is declared. This
extends to structure fields. In C, if you only put
some fields from a structure in a header, then
you will encounter problems when someone tries
to allocate an instance of it on the stack: his
compiler won't allocate enough space for it. Go
packages export the offsets of the public fields.
This allows them to be created and their public
fields accessed from other compilation units.

The example at the start of this section defines
a structure with two fields. The first, a string, is
public and can be accessed from anywhere. The
second, an integer, is private and is only visible
to code in the same package as this definition.
A structure doesn't have to declare any public
fields. You can create *opaque types* by defining a
structure where all of the fields are private.

If you're coming from a class-based language
like C++ or Java, then you may be wondering
why there are public and private fields, but
not protected ones. The answer is quite simple:
there is no inheritance in Go, so protected would
have no meaning. Public and private also have
slightly different meanings in Go and a language
like Java. A private field in a Go structure can
be accessed by any code in the same package,

not just by methods of that structure. If you come from Objective-C, then you can think of private fields in Go structures like `@package` instance variables in Objective-C. If you come from C++, then think of all Go functions in a package as implicitly being friends of all structures declared in the same package.

Defining Methods

```go
9   type integer int
10  func (i integer) log() {
11      fmt.Printf("%d\n", i);
12  }
13  func (e *Example) Log() {
14      e.count++
15      fmt.Printf("%d %s\n", e.count, e.Val)
16  }
```

From: methods.go

If you've used a class-based language, then you are probably wondering why the last example didn't define any methods. defined on the structure. In Go, you may define methods on any concrete type that you define, not just on structures. The example at the start of this section defines two `Log()` methods—recall that the uppercase start letter makes them public— one on the structure defined in the last section and one on a named integer type.

The Go type system lets you assign any `int` to this named type without an explicit cast, but not vice versa. It also prevents you from assigning between two named types. This can be very useful for variables representing quantities. You could, for example, define kilometer and mile types and have the compiler reject any code where you attempted to assign one to the other.

You cannot add methods to existing types— Go does not have an equivalent of Objective-C categories—but you can define new named types and add methods to them.

Methods are declared just like functions, except that there is one extra parameter—the *receiver*—declared before the function name. One of the interesting syntactic quirks of Go is that there is no `this` or `self` keyword. You can give the receiver any name that you want, and this name does not have to be consistent between methods. This idea comes from Oberon-2 and should be popular with people who like the "no magic" philosophy of languages like Objective-C: the receiver is not an implicit hidden parameter that the compiler inserts; it is an explicit parameter just like any other.

The method on the structure in the example at the start of this section takes a pointer as the receiver. This means that it can modify fields of the receiver and these changes will be shared. Methods do not have to take pointers: the other method in the example takes a value. If a method takes a value type, then it can still be called with either a value or a pointer, but it will receive a copy of the structure, so changes that it makes will not be visible from the caller.

When talking about expressions with an explicit type, methods are just functions. You call a method on a structure by using the dot notation, and you declare the parameter that declares how the structure is passed to the method in a special way, but this is just some syntactic sugar. Methods called in this way are semantically equivalent to functions that just take the receiver as an argument: they are statically resolved and are just function calls.

That's not the real power of methods, though. When you call a method via an interface (described in the next section), you get late-bound dynamic lookup. This dual nature of Go methods means that you have a single abstraction that can be used in the same way as either C types or Smalltalk objects. If you require performance, then you can use statically typed definitions and avoid the dynamic lookup. If you require flexibility, then you can use the late binding mechanism of interfaces.

Implementing Interfaces

```go
5   type cartesianPoint struct {
6     x, y float64
7   }
8   type polarPoint struct {
9     r, θ float64
10  }
11
12  func (p cartesianPoint) X() float64 {return p.x }
13  func (p cartesianPoint) Y() float64 {return p.y }
14  func (p polarPoint) X() float64 {
15    return p.r*math.Cos(p.θ)
16  }
17  func (p polarPoint) Y() float64 {
18    return p.r*math.Sin(p.θ)
19  }
20  func (self cartesianPoint) Print() {
21    fmt.Printf("(%f, %f)\n", self.x, self.y)
22  }
23  func (self polarPoint) Print() {
24    fmt.Printf("(%f, %f°)\n", self.r, self.θ)
25  }
26  type Point interface {
27    Printer
28    X() float64
29    Y() float64
30  }
31  type Printer interface {
32    Print()
33  }
```

From: interface.go

The dynamic dispatch mechanism in Go is
reminiscent of StrongTalk, a strongly typed
Smalltalk dialect. Interfaces describe a set of
methods that a type understands. Unlike Java

interfaces or Objective-C protocols, they do not need to be explicitly adopted.

Any type can be assigned to a variable with an interface type, as long as it implements all of the required methods. In some cases, this can be checked at compile time. For example, if one interface is a superset of another, then casting from the superset to the subset is always valid, as is casting from a structure type to an interface when the compiler sees that the structure implements the interface.

In other cases, it is not. These cases require a *type assertion*, detailed in the next section, which will generate a runtime panic if they fail. This means that any variable with an interface type is guaranteed to either be `nil`, or hold a valid value of a concrete type that implements the interface.

The example from the start of this section shows the creation of new structure types, and interfaces that they implement. Note that the structure can be defined before the interface. In fact, structures can be defined in entirely different packages to interfaces. This is especially useful if various third-party structures all implement the same method or group of methods: you can define a new interface that can be any one of them.

There are two interfaces declared in this example, both following Go naming conventions. The `Printer` interface defines a single method,

> **Note:**   If you're coming from C++, then you
> should use interfaces in most of the places where
> you'd use templates in C++. Rather than defining
> template functions or classes (which Go doesn't
> support), define an interface that specifies the set
> of methods that you need, and use it where you
> would use the template parameter in C++.

so it follows the convention of appending the -er
suffix to the method name to give the interface
name.

The other interface uses *interface composition*
to extend the `Printer` interface. This one
defines an abstract data type. It provides
methods for accessing the horizontal and vertical
coordinates of a two-dimensional point. Interface
composition is effectively equivalent to interface
inheritance in Java. You can use it in some
places where you would consider using single or
multiple inheritance in other languages.

This example provides two structures that
implement this interface, one using Cartesian
and the other using polar coordinates. This is a
simple example of how an interface can be used
to hide the implementation. The two structures
both start with lowercase letters, so they will
not be exported from this package, while the
interfaces will. You could extend this example
by providing functions to construct a `Point` from
polar and Cartesian coordinates, each returning

one of a different kind of structure.

When you are dealing with interfaces, the distinction between methods that take pointers and ones that take values becomes more important. If you tried to assign an instance of this example structure to an interface that required the `Log()` method, then the assignment would be rejected. Assigning a pointer to an instance of this structure would work.

This seems counterintuitive. If you have a value, then you can always take its address to get a pointer, so why are the two method sets distinct? The answer is very simple: it helps avoid bugs. When you pass a value, you create a copy of a structure. When you pass a pointer, you alias the structure. If you pass a value and then implicitly, via method invocation on an interface, pass a pointer, then any changes that the method made would be made to the temporary copy, not to the original structure. This is probably not what you want, and if it is then you can just pass the pointer originally, rather than the copy.

The Go FAQ gives an example of a case where this could be problematic:

```
var buf bytes.Buffer
io.Copy(buf, os.Stdin)
```

The `io.Copy()` function copies data from something that implements the `io.Reader` interface to something that implements the `io.Writer` interface. When you call this

function, it will pass a copy of **buf** as the first
argument, because Go always passes by value,
not by reference. It will then try to copy data
from the standard input into the new copy of
buf. When the function returns, the copy of
buf will no longer be referenced, so the garbage
collector will free it.

What the person writing this code probably
wanted to do was copy data from the standard
input into **buf**. The Go type system will
reject this, because **buf** does not implement
the **io.Writer** interface: the method for
writing bytes to a buffer modifies the buffer
and therefore requires a pointer receiver. By
disallowing this, Go lets you get an error at
compile time and trivially fix it by writing this
instead:

```
var buf bytes.Buffer
io.Copy(&buf, os.Stdin)
```

If Go allowed values to use methods that are
declared as requiring a pointer, then you would
instead spend ages wondering why this line
appeared to be reading the correct amount
of data, but wasn't storing any of it in the
buffer that you declared. This is part of the
Go philosophy of avoiding ambiguity. It just
takes one extra character to make a pointer
when you need one. That small amount of extra
effort is a lot less than the time you'd spend
debugging code where you meant one thing and
Go assumed that you meant something else.

Casting Types

```go
 4  type empty interface {}
 5  type example interface {
 6    notImplemented()
 7  }
 8
 9  func main() {
10    one := 1
11    var i empty = one
12    var float float32
13    float = float32(one)
14    switch i.(type) {
15      default:
16        fmt.Printf("Type error!\n")
17      case int:
18        fmt.Printf("%d\n", i)
19    }
20    fmt.Printf("%f\n", float)
21    // This will panic  at run time
22    var e example = i.(example)
23    fmt.Printf("%d\n", e.(empty).(int))
24  }
```

From: cast.go

Unlike C, Go does not allow implicit casting.
This is not laziness on the part of the
implementors: implicit casting makes it easy
for very subtle bugs to slip into code. I recently
had to find a bug in some code that had
gone undetected for several years, where an
implicit cast meant that a value was incorrectly
initialized. The code looked correct, until you
checked the type declarations of everything
involved, which were spread over multiple files.

This is another example of the Go philosophy. You should never need to state the obvious to the compiler, but you should always have to explicitly specify things that are otherwise ambiguous.

The example at the start of this section shows several casts. The concept of casting in other languages is embodied by two concepts in Go. The first is *type conversion*; the second is *type assertion*.

A type conversion is similar to a cast in C. It reinterprets the value as a new type. The conversion from `int` to `float32` is an example of this. The resulting value is a new floating-point value with the same value as the integer. In some cases, the conversion is only approximate. For example, a conversion in the other direction will result in truncation. A type conversion from an integer to a string type will return a single-character string interpreting the integer as a unicode value.

Type assertions are more interesting. They do not convert between types; they simply state to the compiler that the underlying value has the specified type. This assertion is checked at run time. If you try running this example, you will see that it aborts with a runtime panic.

This is because of the type assertion telling the compiler that the type of `i` is something that implements the `example` interface. In fact, the underlying type is `int`, which does

```
1  1
2  1.000000
3  panic: interface conversion: int is not main.
       example: missing method notImplemented
4
5  goroutine 1 [running]:
6  main.main()
7     /Users/theraven/Documents/Books/GoPhrasebook/
          startsnippets/cast.go:22 +0x20d
8
9  goroutine 2 [syscall]:
10 created by runtime.main
11    /Users/theraven/go/src/pkg/runtime/proc.c:219
12 exit status 2
```

Output from: cast.go

not implement the `notImplemented()` method
that this interface specifies. The type check fails
on the type assertion. If you come from C++,
you can think of type assertions as roughly
equivalent to a `dynamic_cast` that throws an
exception[2] on failure.

The final cast-like construct in Go is the *type
switch statement*. This is written like a normal
switch statement, but the switch expression is
a type assertion to **type** and the cases have type
names, rather than values.

The type switch in the example is used as a
simple type check, like a C++ `dynamic_cast`.

---

[2]Runtime panics are not quite analogous to C++
exceptions. The differences are covered in Chapter 8,
Handling Errors.

It is more common to use type switches when
defining generic data structures (see Chapter 4,
Common Go Patterns) to allow special cases for
various types.

Numbers

When I first learned C, the compiler supported 16-bit `int`s and 32-bit `long`s. A few years later, it became more common for `int` to be 32 bits. A lot of code was written with assumptions about the sizes of C types, and this caused people a lot of problems when 64-bit systems became common.

The C99 standard introduced the `stdint.h` header, which defined types like `uint32_t`, an unsigned integer that was 32 bits on any platform. This helped a bit, but on some platforms a cast between a `uint32_t` and an `unsigned int` was safe and wouldn't generate a warning, since they were the same underlying type, while on others it was not.

Go learned from this mess and provides explicitly sized integer and floating-point types from the start. A `uint64` is always a 64-bit unsigned integer. An `int16` is always a 16-bit signed integer.

Sometimes, you don't want to specify the
exact size of a type. Go also provides `int` and
`uint` types, which have more or less the same
definition as in C. They are a natural size for the
machine, but always at least 32 bits.[1] Unlike
the C equivalent, you cannot implicitly cast
between `int` and any explicitly sized type. This
avoids the case where code is performing a safe
conversion on one platform but not on another.

Converting Between Strings and Numbers

```
1  package main
2  import "fmt"
3  import "strconv"
4
5  func main() {
6      var i int
7      fmt.Scanf("%d", &i)
8      str := strconv.FormatInt(int64(i), 10)
9      hex, _ := strconv.ParseInt(str, 16, 64)
10     fmt.Printf("%d\n", hex)
11 }
```

From: str2num.go

We've already seen some examples of converting
between numbers and strings using the *fmt
package.* You can use numerical format specifiers
with functions like **Printf()** and **Scanf()** to

[1]Go does not currently support any 16-bit
architectures, and probably never will.

read and write numbers, but that's often overkill for a simple conversion.

The *strconv package* contains various functions to just perform the conversions. These allow conversion between numerical types and strings, in both directions, optionally with a specified number base.

The example at the start of this section shows a rather convoluted sequence of conversions. This first reads some characters from the standard input, which it interprets as a decimal integer. It then constructs a string from this, and then parses the string as a base-16 integer. Finally, it outputs the value as a base-10 integer again.

Prior to Go 1.0, the functions in this package had quite confusing names for various number bases. Now the large range of functions has been replaced by a simpler set of more generic ones. The example uses `FormatInt()` to create a string from the integer and `ParseInt()` to perform the inverse conversion.

We're ignoring the second value returned from `strconv.ParseInt()`. This is an error value, and we assume that the input is always valid. If you are getting the string from user input then you should probably check the error value.

Using Large Integers

```go
package main
import "math/big"
import "fmt"

func main() {
  var n int
  fmt.Printf("Compute how many Fibonacci numbers? ")
  fmt.Scanf("%d", &n)
  last := big.NewInt(1)
  current := big.NewInt(1)
  for i := 0 ; (i < n) && (i < 2) ; i++ {
    fmt.Printf("1\n")
  }
  for i := 2 ; i < n ; i++ {
    last.Add(last, current)
    tmp := last
    last = current
    current = tmp
    fmt.Printf("%s\n", current.String())
  }
}
```

From: fib.go

The *math/big package* defines two types: one for arbitrary-length integers and one for arbitrary-size rational numbers, represented as fractions. These each define a set of operations, all following the same general, slightly unintuitive, form.

Operations such as Add are methods on these types. The receiver is set to the result of performing the operation on the two operands and returned. This means that a.Add(b,c) on

a type from the big package is equivalent to
a = b + c on built-in numeric types.

The example at the start of this section shows
how to use big integers to compute the Fibonacci
sequence. This program creates two big integers,
one for each of the last two values in the
sequence.

There is no explicit typing in this program
(except for the small integer used for the loop).
This is one of the nice things about Go: you
rarely have to worry about types; you can rely
on type inference everywhere. The three big
integers are all pointers to big int structures.
One of the advantages of garbage collection is
that you don't have to care about this. Variables
will automatically be cleaned up whether they
are pointer or structure types.

A big integer implementation of any kind will
need to store an arbitrary amount of data, so
it's more efficient if we reuse them. To compute
the sequence, we just add the last two values
together and then loop, discarding the old
last value implicitly in the addition and then
swapping them.

The swap operation is very cheap, because they
are pointer types: we are just changing how we
refer to the two objects, not copying them.

Converting Between Numbers and Pointers

```go
package main
import "fmt"
import "unsafe"

func main() {
  str := "A Go variable"
  addr := unsafe.Pointer(&str)
  fmt.Printf("The address of str is %d\n", addr)
  str2 := (*string)(addr)
  fmt.Printf("String constructed from pointer: %s
    \n", *str2)
  address := uintptr(addr)
  address += 4
  // This has undefined behavior!
  str3 := (*string)(unsafe.Pointer(address))
  fmt.Printf("String constructed from pointer: %s
    \n", *str3)
}
```

From: ptr2int.go

In BCPL, there was no distinction between integer and pointer types; there was just a single word type, which stored a value that could fit in a register. If you did some arithmetic on such a value, it was treated as an integer; if you dereferenced it then it was treated as a pointer.

C added some explicit typing, so integers and pointers were treated as distinct types, but still allowed implicit conversions between pointers and pointer-sized integers. It also allowed various forms of arithmetic on pointers. In C, a pointer is just a number representing an address in memory, with a small amount of type checking to prevent you from doing some of the more obviously stupid things that it's possible to do with pointers.

In Go, pointers and integers are completely distinct types. Converting between them is supported via the *unsafe package*, as shown in the example at the start of this section.

Note: Unsafe operations are not always supported. Passing the -u flag to the Go compiler disables it. This is commonly used in hosted Go environments, including the Google App Engine.

The first thing that you should notice about this example is that it is convoluted and verbose. This is intentional: doing low-level things with pointers is very rarely the correct thing to do, and Go doesn't want to encourage this kind of behavior. In C, you often have to do pointer arithmetic because the language doesn't provide a sensible way of doing what you want. In Go, you commonly only need to access pointers as integers for interfacing with other languages, or for some very low-level tasks. Abstractions like slices avoid the need in common cases.

The unsafe package provides a `Pointer` type, which represents an arbitrary pointer. This has some special properties. It can be cast to and from a `uintptr`, giving a numerical value representing the address. It can also be cast to and from any other Go pointer type. This completely bypasses the type checking mechanisms in Go, and so there is no guarantee that the resulting pointer is valid.

The example first converts the pointer back to its original type. It then does some invalid pointer arithmetic and tries to convert the result to a string pointer, which it then dereferences.

If you try running this example, then it may exit normally after showing some random value for the last two statements, but it is more likely to abort with a runtime panic delivered as a result of receiving a segmentation fault signal.

Don't let the panic mislead you into thinking that Go will always catch this error. Sometimes this will appear to work correctly but give you bizarre results. The unsafe package is correctly named: It allows you to do unsafe things. Unlike C, Go makes it explicit when you are doing potentially unsafe things with pointers.

```
1   The address of str is 0x421310a0
2   String constructed from pointer: A Go variable
3   unexpected fault address 0xd00000000
4   throw: fault
5   [signal 0xb code=0x1 addr=0xd00000000 pc=0x17053]
6
7   goroutine 1 [running]:
8   bytes.(*Buffer).WriteString(0x4214e008, 0
        xd00000000, 0x6f472041, 0xd, 0x0, ...)
9     go/src/pkg/bytes/buffer.go:119 +0x9d
10  fmt.(*fmt).padString(0x4214e098, 0xd00000000, 0
        x6f472041, 0xd00000000)
11    go/src/pkg/fmt/format.go:140 +0xe8
12  fmt.(*fmt).fmt_s(0x4214e098, 0xd00000000, 0
        x6f472041, 0x57770)
13    go/src/pkg/fmt/format.go:287 +0x60
14  fmt.(*pp).fmtString(0x4214e000, 0xd00000000, 0
        x6f472041, 0x73, 0x6f472041, ...)
15    go/src/pkg/fmt/print.go:504 +0xb8
16  fmt.(*pp).printField(0x4214e000, 0x57770, 0
        x42131080, 0x73, 0x0, ...)
17    go/src/pkg/fmt/print.go:744 +0xa47
18  fmt.(*pp).doPrintf(0x4214e000, 0x9ebf4, 0
        x400000024, 0x442148f70, 0x100000001, ...)
19    go/src/pkg/fmt/print.go:1046 +0x7b0
20  fmt.Fprintf(0x4212ea50, 0x42148008, 0x9ebf4, 0x24
        , 0x442148f70, ...)
21    go/src/pkg/fmt/print.go:181 +0x7c
22  fmt.Printf(0x9ebf4, 0x6972745300000024, 0
        x442148f70, 0x100000001, 0x42131080, ...)
23    go/src/pkg/fmt/print.go:190 +0x97
24  main.main()
25    ptr2int.go:15 +0x1ea
26
27  goroutine 2 [syscall]:
28  created by runtime.main
29    go/src/pkg/runtime/proc.c:219
30  exit status 2
```

Output from: ptr2int.go

Common Go Patterns

The first step to fluent use of any programming language is understanding the design patterns and idioms that are commonly used. Learning the syntax is only the first step to learning how to think in the language, akin to learning vocabulary and basic grammar in a natural language. People speaking a second language often make very amusing mistakes by literally translating idioms from their first language.

Programming languages are no different. If you've read C++ code written by Java programmers, or vice versa, then you've probably encountered this. Just translating an approach that you would use in one language into another will work (as long as both languages are equally expressive), but it will usually give horrible code.

Design patterns in a programming language

are like the idioms of a natural language. Some work in a lot of languages; others don't. Quite often, you will find that design patterns in one language work around a missing feature. For example, *resource acquisition is initialization (RAII)* is a common C++ idiom, yet it makes no sense in a garbage-collected language because object lifetimes are not related to their scopes. Better techniques (such as Go's **defer** statement) exist to solve the same problem. Go, like every other language, has a set of common patterns that are not necessarily applicable elsewhere.

Zero Initialization

```
5   type Logger struct {
6      out *os.File
7   }
8
9   func (l Logger) Log(s string) {
10     out := l.out
11     if (out == nil) {
12        out = os.Stderr
13     }
14     fmt.Fprintf(out, "%s [%d]: %s\n", os.Args[0],
              os.Getpid(), s)
15  }
16
17  func (l *Logger) SetOutput(out *os.File) {
18     l.out = out
19  }
```

From: log.go
One of the important concepts in Go is the *zero*

value. When you declare a new variable, or
when you create a value with the **new()** built-
in function, it is initialized to the zero value for
the type.

As its name implies, the zero value is the value
when all of the memory used by the type is filled
with zeros. It is common for Go data types to be
expected to work with their zero value, without
any further initialization. For example, the zero
value for a Go mutex is an unlocked mutex: you
just need to create the memory for it and it's
ready to use. Similarly, the zero value for an
arbitrary-precision integer in Go represents the
value zero.

In other languages, the *two-stage creation
pattern* is common. This separates the allocation
and initialization of objects into two explicit
steps. In Go, there is no support for explicitly
managing memory. If you declare a local variable
and then take its address, or declare a pointer
and use **new()** to create an object that it points
to, the compiler is likely to generate the same
code. The way in which you declare an object is
a hint to the compiler, not an instruction. There
is therefore little point in supporting two-stage
creation in Go.

The second stage is also often redundant. An
initializer that takes no arguments should not
have to be stated. The fact that it can be
commonly leads to bugs.

A concrete example of this is the POSIX thread

API mutex. On FreeBSD, this is a pointer and a NULL value will be implicitly initialized. With the GNU/Linux implementation, it is a structure, and using an uninitialized version has undefined behavior. The compiler, however, has no way of knowing the difference between an initialized and an uninitialized mutex, so it will not give any warnings. A program that forgets to initialize the mutex can compile without any warnings, even at the highest warning level, and it may work sometimes, but it will fail unpredictably on some platforms.

In Go, this kind of bug is very rare. The common structures all use the zero initialization pattern, which means that you can always use a newly created instance of them immediately. The only time that you need to explicitly initialize one is when you want something other than the default behavior.

The same is true of other types. A pointer in Go is always initialized to nil, unless explicitly initialized to point to a valid object. In contrast, a pointer in C declared as a local value can contain any value. It may point to a live variable, or to an invalid memory address.

The Go approach has several advantages. First, there is no need for the compiler to perform complex flow analysis to warn you that a variable might be used uninitialized: there is no such thing as an uninitialized variable. This sounds simple, but determining if a variable may be used before being initialized is nontrivial, and modern C compilers still don't always get it right. Secondly, it simplifies code. You only ever explicitly initialize a variable when you want to then use the value that you assigned to it.

You should aim to support this pattern in any Go structures that you define. Usually, this is easy. If your structure contains other structures as fields, and these structures support this pattern, then you get support for free.

If you are relying on other values, then it can be more complex. This is especially true with pointers: They do not support the zero initialization pattern. If you call a method on a nil pointer then you will get a crash unless the method is careful not to dereference the pointer.

The example at the start of this section shows one way of implementing the zero initialization pattern for structures that contain pointers. This example defines a structure for generating log messages and sending them to a file. The zero structure implicitly uses the standard error file descriptor, rather than a file stored in the structure.

Note that we are not setting the **out** field in the structure to anything; if it is not set, we are just using a different value. There are two reasons for this. The first is largely aesthetic: it lets us tell the difference between a **Logger** that is writing to the standard output because it has been explicitly set to use the standard output, and one that is using it implicitly. In this particular example, it's not very important, but in other cases it can be.

The other reason is that it means that this method does not need to take a pointer to the structure. This is quite important because of how it relates to the Go type system. If you call a method via an interface, then methods that accept a pointer are only callable if the interface variable contains a pointer.

For example, you could define an interface that defined the `Log()` method and create a variable of this type. Then you could assign an instance of the **Logger** structure to that variable. You could also assign a pointer to an instance of the **Logger** structure to this variable. Both would work, because the `Log()` method is callable from both instances of the structure and pointers to instances. If the method took a pointer argument, then you would only be able to call it on pointers. It's therefore good style in Go to only require methods to take a pointer when they modify the structure, or if the structure is so large that copying it on every method call would be prohibitive.

Generic Data Structures

```
4   type stackEntry struct{
5     next *stackEntry
6     value interface{}
7   }
8   type stack struct {
9     top *stackEntry
10  }
11
12  func (s *stack) Push(v interface{}) {
13    var e stackEntry
14    e.value = v
15    e.next = s.top
16    s.top = &e
17  }
18  func (s *stack) Pop() interface{} {
19    if s.top == nil {
20      return nil
21    }
22    v := s.top.value
23    s.top = s.top.next
24    return v
25  }
```

From: genericStack.go

The *empty interface type* is a very important
part of the Go type system. This has a similar,
although slightly more generic, place to
void* in C: It can represent any type. The
empty interface literally means "any type that
implements—at the least—no methods," a
restriction matched by every type.

It is common to use the empty interface type in
generic data structures. If you can store values
of the generic interface type, then you can store

values of any type. You can't, however, perform any operations on them.

If you want to create something like a set, then you must define a mechanism for defining equality, which typically involves defining an interface with an `isEqual()` method or something similar. If you are creating a data structure that doesn't need to be aware of the representation or semantics of the values that it contains, then you should use the empty interface.

The example at the start of this section shows a generic stack type, with `Push()` and `Pop()` methods, capable of storing any Go type. The implementation is very simple: a singly-linked list of a private structure type that stores a value.

You can use the same technique when creating far more complex data structures. The advantage of using the empty interface type is that it allows both structure and primitive types to be stored. In the next section, we'll look at how you can extend this general approach and specialize it for specific types.

Specialized Generic Data Structures

```go
31  func (s *stack) pushInt(v int64) {
32    if (s.isInteger) {
33      top := s.top.(*integerStackEntry)
34      if top.value == v {
35        top.count++
36        return
37      }
38    }
39    var e integerStackEntry
40    e.value = v
41    e.next = s.top
42    s.top = &e
43    s.isInteger = true
44  }
45  func (s *stack) Push(v interface{}) {
46    switch val := v.(type) {
47      case int64: s.pushInt(val)
48      case int: s.pushInt(int64(val))
49      default:
50        var e genericStackEntry
51        e.value = v
52        e.next = s.top
53        s.top = &e
54        s.isInteger = false
55    }
56  }
```

From: specializedStack.go

Suppose you wanted to use the stack from
the last section in a push-down automaton.
You'd probably be mainly pushing and popping
integers, and often pushing the same integer
several times in a row. There's a large potential

for optimization: you can have a specialized version of the stack entry that stores an integer and a count. If you push the same integer twice, then you just increment the count, saving the overhead of an allocation.

The example at the start of this section shows an expanded **Push()** method that does this. This now uses two types: one for the generic case and one for the integer case.

```
4   type stackEntry interface {
5     pop() (interface{}, stackEntry)
6   }
7   type genericStackEntry struct {
8     next stackEntry
9     value interface{}
10  }
11  func (g genericStackEntry) pop() (interface{},
       stackEntry) {
12    return g.value, g.next
13  }
14  type integerStackEntry struct {
15    value int64
16    count int
17    next stackEntry
18  }
19  func (i *integerStackEntry) pop() (interface{},
       stackEntry) {
20    if (i.count > 0) {
21      i.count--
22      return i.value, i
23    }
24    return i.value, i.next
25  }
```

From: specializedStack.go

When you push an integer, it uses a type switch statement to determine the type, and checks whether the last value to be pushed was an integer and if it has the same value as the top value. In this case, it just increments the count.

This example splits the specialized work up a bit between the generic data structure and the specialized components. You might want to modify it to add a `tryPush()` method to the `stackEntry` interface, which would try to add the value without adding a new stack entry. If this failed, then you could allocate a new entry of the same type.

This pattern shows one of the big advantages of the loose coupling that Go provides. The interface to the stack that uses a combination of `genericStackEntry` and `integerStackEntry` structures for its elements is completely compatible with the one from the last section, but is now more efficient for storing large sequences of identical integer values. The details of the two concrete structures implementing stack entries are completely hidden.

You can use this same approach to implement generic collections and then specialize them for your data. Complex collections in languages like Go typically incorporate this kind of self-optimizing behavior.

This is a fairly simple example and the saving in this case is not particularly worthwhile. If you were implementing a real stack, then a slice of empty interfaces would almost certainly be a lot faster and use less memory. The point of this example is to show you the general pattern, not how to write an efficient stack in Go.

This pattern is very useful in more complex data structures. For example, the underlying implementation of the map types uses a similar technique, generating a hash value based on the underlying type. You might want to do something similar, providing a built-in hash for basic types, using a zero hash by default, or using the **Hash()** method if one exists.

Implementation Hiding

```
27    type Stack interface {
28      Push(interface{})
29      Pop() interface{}
30    }
31    func NewStack() Stack {
32      return &stack{}
33    }
```

From: genericStack.go

Interfaces in Go are exactly what their name implies. They define how you interact with a type, not how it is implemented. If users of your structure do not need to be able to access any of the fields, then it is good style to only export an interface exposing the public methods, rather than the structure itself.

The example at the start of this section shows a public interface for the two stack structures that we've defined already this chapter, along with a function for constructing it. By convention, the function that creates the concrete instance is named `NewSomething()`, if `Something` is the name of the interface.

This is not the only way of hiding implementation details. Any structure member that does not start with a capital letter is automatically hidden, and is only accessible from within the package in which it is declared. As such, the structures that we've defined to implement the stacks are already hiding the details of their implementation: none of their fields is visible from other packages.

The correct approach to use depends on how you expect people to use your structures. Only exporting the interface gives you the most flexibility, because you can completely change any details of the implementation without altering code that uses it. You can even implement several different structures optimized for different use cases and return different ones depending on the use. On the other hand, this approach prevents people from allocating instances of your structure on the stack, and prevents you from using the *zero initialization pattern*.

Although Go does not support explicit stack allocation, the compiler will try to allocate structures on the stack as an implementation detail if they are short-lived and do not have their address taken. This is very fast, as it just requires modifying the value of a register: variables on the stack are allocated just by moving the stack pointer. If the object is returned as a pointer via a constructor function, then the compiler is unable to do this, and will need to request memory that is managed by the garbage collector. For short-lived structures, this can be a significant performance penalty.

Type Embedding

```go
4   type A struct {}
5   type B struct {}
6   func (_ A) Print() { fmt.Printf("A printed\n") }
7   func (_ B) Print() { fmt.Printf("B printed\n") }
8   func (a A) PrintA() { a.Print() }
9   type C struct {
10      A
11      *B
12  }
13  func main() {
14      var c C
15      c.B = &B{}
16      // Implicitly inherited
17      c.PrintA()
18      // Not allowed: ambiguous
19      // c.Print()
20      // Explicitly disambiguated
21      c.B.Print()
22      c.A.Print()
23  }
```

From: embed.go

Go doesn't support subclassing, but it is possible to achieve something similar via the limited form of implicit delegation that Go does support.

If you make an unnamed field in a Go structure, then any methods defined by the type of the field are implicitly added to the enclosing structure. The example at the start of this section contains a structure C that has two unnamed fields: fields with a type (A and B*), but with no name.

Note that the receiver for any of these methods

will be the field, not the outer structure. This means that, even if the receiver is a pointer, it is not possible for it to access any of the fields in the outer structure. This can be slightly inconvenient. For example, it would be useful to be able to provide a `List` structure that could be added to any structure that needed list behavior, adding a `Next()` method returning the next item in the list, but this is not possible.

The example at the start of this section shows a problem that can occur when embedding structures in this way: What happens when two inner structures implement the same methods? There are lots of ways of solving this problem, including priority schemes, which can get very complicated with multiple layers of nesting.

Note: There is no direct Go equivalent of a C++ virtual base class. If a Go structure contains structures A and B as fields, and each of these contains an instance of a C as a field, then the outer structure will always contain two instances of C. It is possible to achieve something similar by making A and B contain a pointer to C, and explicitly setting them to point to the same instance.

The Go solution is to make programmers explicitly specify what they mean. Calling `c.Print()` in this example (the commented-out line) would cause the compiler to reject the program: it can't figure out which `Print()` method you really mean without potentially introducing bugs into your program. You could extend this example by adding an explicit `Print()` method to `C` that delegated to one of the fields, or implemented the method in some other way.

Note that this example uses both a pointer and a value as fields, but the methods work on both. Exactly the same rules for methods apply in this case. The pointer field will add methods that take a value or a pointer, and the value field will add methods that take the value.

Arrays and Slices

Almost every programming language has a data structure that it calls an array, but the exact semantics vary considerably. In some languages, an array is a dynamically resizeable ordered collection of objects. In others, it's a block of memory, with some vague hint that it probably contains variables of a specific type.

In Go, arrays are a very low-level data structure. Like C arrays, they are simply blocks of memory, but there are some important differences. Remember that Go does not permit pointer arithmetic. In C, array subscripting is just another way of writing pointer arithmetic, and you can use array and pointer types almost interchangeably.

In Go, pointers and arrays are distinct types. Because arrays and pointers are distinct, there is no such thing in Go as an arbitrary-sized array. The size of a Go array is intrinsic to its type. An array of 10 integers is a different type than an array of 5 integers.

One side effect of this is that there is automatic bounds checking with Go arrays. In C, you can trivially allocate an array of 10 elements, cast it to a pointer, access elements beyond the end of the array, and end up with undefined behavior.

```
package main
import "fmt"
func main() {
  var a [2]int
  for i := 0 ; i<15 ; i++ {
    fmt.Printf("Element: %d %d\n", i, a[i])
  }
}
```

From: overflow.go

The overflow.go example shows a simple Go program that declares a small array and then tries to access past the end of it. The compiler doesn't catch this as a static type error, because it isn't doing enough range analysis to know that the index variable extends past the end of the array. The runtime system, however, does catch it.

```
Element: 0 0
Element: 1 0
panic: runtime error: index out of range
```

Output from: overflow.go

When you run this example, you get a runtime *panic*, which we'll look at in more detail in Chapter 8, *Handling Errors*. This is a recoverable runtime error. A similar program in C would just silently access a random stack location. If you assigned to the variable, the C version would corrupt the stack, while the Go version would give you a helpful error.

Note that this is not a sensible idiom for iterating over an array. We'll look at a better way of doing so later.

Creating Arrays

```
4   var a1 [100]int
5   var matrix [4][4]float64
6   a2 := [...]int{1, 1, 2, 3, 5}
```

From: array.go

As mentioned earlier, the type of a Go array is a combination of its size and the type of its elements. This means that the size of the array must be known at compile time. That does not mean that it must be explicit. The third form of array declaration in the example at the start of this section shows how to create an array whose size is inferred. This creates an array of five integers, with a static type of `[5]int`.

Arrays can contain any types, including other arrays. The middle example creates an array of arrays of floating-point values. All arrays are values. If you assign from one array to another, you get a copy of the array.

```
1  package main
2  import "fmt"
3
4  func main() {
5    a1 := [...]int{1, 2}
6    a2 := a1
7    a2[0] = 3
8    fmt.Printf("%d %d\n", a1[0], a2[0])
9  }
```

From: arrayAssign.go

Contrast this with C, where you can treat the name of the array as a pointer to its first element. This highlights an important philosophical difference between C and Go.

```
1  1 3
```

Output from: arrayAssign.go

Copying an array is potentially very slow: it's a linear time operation. Assigning a pointer, in contrast, is a very fast operation. C favors the fast operation by making it the default and requiring the programmer to explicitly state when he wants the slow operation.

Aliasing a data structure is fast, but it's also a very common source of bugs, especially in concurrent code. Go, therefore, defaults to copying. Go makes it *possible* to write fast code, but makes it *easy* to write correct code. This is the opposite of the C philosophy, which makes it easy to write fast code and possible to write correct code.

Slicing Arrays

```
4    var a1 [100]int
5    firstHalf := a1[:50]
6    secondHalf := a1[50:]
7    middle := a1[25:75]
8    all := a1[:]
```

From: slice.go

If you've looked at any C code, you'll have noticed a common idiom: passing a pointer and a length as arguments to a function. This allows you to pass an array of an arbitrary size to a function. The downside of this approach is that it's entirely informal. A typo can easily make you pass the wrong size, and then you're back to memory corruption.

In Go, a much cleaner replacement for this idiom is formalized in the language. Rather than passing an array, or a pointer to the array, you pass a *slice*. A slice is a view on an array. If you've written JavaScript code with the WebGL extension, then this will be familiar to you: Go slices are conceptually similar to ArrayBufferView objects, while Go arrays are similar to ArrayBuffers.

If you compile with gccgo, then you can inspect the implementation of a slice easily. It's just a C structure that stores a pointer to the array, its size, and its capacity.

Note: Slices have both a size and a capacity. The size is the number of array elements that you can access from that slice. The capacity is the maximum size slice that you can make by extending that slice, which is at most the size of the underlying array but may be less if you are using slices to restrict access to a range within an array. You can often ignore the capacity.

Slices are often used as function call parameters, because their size is a dynamic property, rather than an attribute of the type. If you use an array type as a function parameter, then the size is embedded in the type and callers can't pass a larger array. If you use a slice type, then the caller can pass a reference to any size of memory allocation and the callee can test that it's adequate.

There are other uses for slices. For example, you can use them to provide restricted range checking on an array. This can be a useful way of adding some sanity checking: use a slice of the array rather than the entire array and you can make sure that you didn't accidentally exceed the bounds you thought were the limit.

The syntax for creating slices from arrays (or other slices) is shown at the start of this section. Slices are created from ranges in existing arrays or slices, with the start and end indexes separated by a colon. If either of the indexes is omitted, then the slice extends to that end. As with most modern languages, Go arrays and slices are indexed from zero.

Resizing Slices

```go
func main() {
    s0 := make([]int, 2, 10)
    s1 := append(s0, 2)
    s2 := append(s0, 3)
    fmt.Printf("Element: %d %d\n", s1[2], s2[2])
    s0 = []int{0, 1}
    s1 = append(s0, 2)
    s2 = append(s0, 3)
    fmt.Printf("Element: %d %d\n", s1[2], s2[2])
}
```

From: expandSlice.go

Resizing a slice is something of a misnomer. A slice itself is an immutable. You can't expand a slice, but you can create a new slice that is a larger reference to the same array, or to a new, larger, array containing the same values.

It's very important to be aware of exactly which of these operations you are preforming. Consider the example at the start of this section. It performs the same two **append()** operations on two different slices, both with the same size, but with very different results.

```
1   Element: 3 3
2   Element: 2 3
```

Output from: expandSlice.go

The first slice has two elements, but a capacity of 10. This means that it is backed by an array of 10 elements, and just refers to the first two. The **append()** operation will create a new slice pointing to the same array, and set the next element in the array. The second **append()** operation does exactly the same thing. Slices **s1** and **s2** are both referencing the same underlying array, and the creation of **s2** modified **s1**.

The slice created with the **[]int{0, 1}** initializer has a capacity of two. The two **append()** operations now create a new array, copy the contents of the array that backs **s0** into it, and then set the third element.

You have to be very careful to think about aliasing when you use slices. If you have multiple slices referencing overlapping sections of a single array, then changes in one will be reflected in the others. Usually when you're using slices, this is what you want.

Truncating Slices

```go
3    func truncate(slice []int) []int {
4      var s []int = make([]int, len(slice))
5      copy(s, slice)
6      return s
7    }
```

From: sliceShrink.go

Slices are just views on arrays. This means that
they are very cheap to create; you just have to
allocate a few words of memory describing the
range within the array. This is a constant-time
operation, independent of the size of the slice. In
contrast, creating a copy of the array is a linear
time operation, and so usually best avoided.

Quite often, you will use a slice for a dynamic
buffer and, after a sequence of operations, end
up with a small slice pointing to a large array.
When this happens, it's tempting to just use the
small slice and forget about the large array.

Unfortunately, because slices refer to entire
arrays, this means that the garbage collector will
ensure that the array is not freed until the slice
has been freed. If you allocate a 10MB array,
it will remain in memory even if the only thing
referencing it is a slice pointing to a one-value
range.

The example at the start of this section shows
a function that creates a new slice, backed by
a new array, and then truncates it. If you use
the result of this function, instead of the slice

that you pass as an argument, the GC is free to delete the original array.

Be careful with the advice in this section. It's tempting to fall prey to premature optimization and aggressively copy arrays. Always be aware of the lifespan of your new slice if you're doing this. There's no point copying a chunk of data just to allow the GC to collect an array a few milliseconds earlier. As always, profile first, and optimize second.

Iterating Over Arrays

```go
package main
import "fmt"
import "time"
func main() {
  var a [100]int
  // The slow way
  for i := 1 ; i < 10 ; i++ {
    fmt.Printf("Element %d is %d\n", i, a[i])
  }
  // The fast way
  subrange := a[1:10]
  for i, v := range subrange {
    fmt.Printf("Element: %d %d\n", i, v)
  }
  // The parallel way
  for i, v := range subrange {
    go fmt.Printf("Element: %d %d\n", i, v)
  }
  time.Sleep(10000000)
}
```

From: iterate.go

A few years ago, some researchers at IBM discovered that one of the main reasons for Java code being slower than C was the cost of bounds checking. Iterating over all of the elements in an array is a very common idiom in any language. In C, this is implemented just by adding the size of an element to a pointer value. In Java, and other high-level languages, it requires checking that the pointer value is in range as well.

A lot of research effort has gone into trying to remove these run-time bounds checks, but it's not a trivial problem in the general case. You can improve performance a lot by helping the compiler and using idioms that allow it to perform the bounds check once per loop, rather than once per iteration.

The example at the start of this section shows three ways of iterating over part of an array. The first is a C-like way of doing it. The second is more idiomatic Go. Note the use of a slice to define a range within the array for iteration. You can use the entire array here in exactly the same way, but defining a slice allows you to iterate over a range within the array quickly and easily.

The third approach is the most interesting. This iterates over the array, with each loop iteration running in a separate goroutine. This pattern is most useful if you are doing a fairly significant amount of work with each element in the array.

More commonly, you'd want to mix these approaches. If you want to process a lot of elements in an array, then you can use slices to split it up into smaller chunks and then use a concurrent goroutine for each of the slices.

Manipulating Strings

C was created in America, back when it was fashionable to pretend that the rest of the world didn't exist, so it used 7-bit ASCII[1] characters to represent strings.

Go is more recent, and since then most technology companies in the USA have discovered that it's quite a good idea to support other languages, mostly so you can sell things to people in other countries. Go uses UTF-8. This is entirely unsurprising, as UTF-8 was originally designed (on a diner placemat) by Rob Pike and Ken Thompson, two of the designers of Go.

Go strings are slightly higher-level than

---

[1] American Standard Code for Information Interchange, a format based on the assumption that there was no need to interchange information with people who used accents on letters, non-Latin characters, or currencies other than dollars.

C strings, and there are some important
differences. The most obvious is that the Go
string type is immutable, like C constant strings
and Java strings. Although strings behave very
much like arrays, they are a separate type, with
their own unique behavior. In some cases, you
can treat a string as an array (or, rather, a slice)
of bytes, while in others the fact that it contains
Unicode character data becomes important.

Comparing Strings

```
5   str1 := "A string"
6   str2 := "A " + "string"
7   if (str1 == str2) {
8      fmt.Printf("'%s' and '%s' are equal\n", str1,
          str2)
9   }
10  if (&str1 == &str2) {
11     fmt.Printf("'%s' and '%s' are identical\n",
          str1, str2)
12  }
13  str2 += " with a suffix"
14  if (str1 < str2) {
15     fmt.Printf("'%s' comes before '%s'\n", str1,
          str2)
16  }
```

From: compareStrings.go

Go strings are a high-level type, and have the
concept of equality built in. A large percentage
of bugs in C code relate to the handling of
strings, and fixing this was one of the important
tasks when designing Go.

This is obvious when you look at comparing strings in the two languages. In C, a string is just a pointer to some bytes somewhere in memory. In Go, it is a real data type, built on the same low-level abstraction, but providing a more human-friendly interface.

When you use the normal comparison operators in Go, you get a result that makes sense considering the semantic content of the string. If two strings have the same character contents, they are considered equal. The less-than and greater-than operators will return an ordering based on their lexical ordering.

Unfortunately, this highlights one of the areas in which Go is currently very weak: localization. Strings are ordered based on the Unicode values of their constituent characters. In some locales, this is correct, but in others it is not. For example, the ordering between E and É is highly dependent on the locale. In some, they should be together, but in other locales, accented characters come after all non-accented characters. Go does not currently provide any locale-aware means of sorting strings. In C++, you could use operator overloading to define a new string type that supported locale-aware sorting. The lack of operator overloading in Go makes this impossible.

Note: Go is under constant development, so
just because certain functionality doesn't exist at
the time of writing does not mean that it won't
exist by the time you read this. Check the Go
package directory (http://golang.org/pkg/)
for locale support; it may have been added since
publication.

Processing a String One Character at a Time

```go
4   func main() {
5     str := "Étoilé"
6     // Don't do this!
7     for i := 0 ; i<len(str) ; i++ {
8       fmt.Printf("%c", str[i])
9     }
10    fmt.Printf("\n")
11    // Do this instead
12    for _, c := range str {
13      fmt.Printf("%c", c)
14    }
15    fmt.Printf("\n")
16  }
```

From: stringIterate.go

The naïve way of iterating over the characters
in a string would be to use a **for** loop indexing
each character. This almost works, but it
iterates over every byte, not every character.

UTF-8 is a way of encoding Unicode characters.
There are several different encodings for

Unicode, with UTF-8 and UTF-16 being the two most common. Both of these are *multibyte character encodings*, meaning that one character may be represented by more than one byte. In fact, they are both variable-length encodings as well. The 8 and 16 in their names refer to the number of bits in the smallest encodings.

A character encoded in UTF-8 is somewhere between one and four bytes long, depending on the character. The 128 ASCII characters are all single bytes, while other characters are longer.

If you iterate over a string using byte indexes, then your code may work. Only one of the characters in this section so far has had a multibyte encoding in UTF-8: the ï in naïve. Without that, it would be perfectly safe to treat this entire section as ASCII when manipulating it. If English is your native language, then it's very easy to test code dealing with strings with input data that looks representative, and then have it break the first time someone else uses it.

```
1  ÃtoilÃ©
2  Étoilé
```

Output from: stringIterate.go

Fortunately, there is another alternative. The standard Go iteration pattern also works on strings. This returns each character, as a 32-bit integer representing a single Unicode character.

Even this isn't quite correct. Unicode supports
the idea of *composed characters*, where a single
character is defined by a sequence of code points.
Fortunately, unless you are writing a text layout
engine, it's almost always safe to ignore these.

Processing a Partial String One Character at a Time

```go
package main
import "fmt"
import "unicode/utf8"

func main() {
  str := "Étoilé"
  rune := make([]byte, 0, 4)
  for i := 0 ; i<len(str) ; i++ {
    rune = append(rune, str[i])
    if (utf8.FullRune(rune)) {
      char, _ := utf8.DecodeRune(rune)
      fmt.Printf("%c", char)
      rune = rune[0:0]
    }
  }
  fmt.Printf("\n")
}
```

From: partialStringIterate.go

When you have a complete string in memory,
it's easy to iterate over it, but what happens
when you are receiving text from the network,
or reading it from the disk? In both cases, you
will typically end up with buffers full of bytes in
UTF-8 format.

With ASCII data, this wouldn't be a problem. One byte means one character. With UTF-8, a single byte may be a character, or it may be the first byte in a multibyte character. The *unicode/utf8 package* provides some helpful functions for telling these two apart.

The example from the start of this section uses a static string, but the same code would work on a stream of bytes acquired from any source. It collects the bytes into a short buffer until they represent a complete character, and then decodes them.

This is quite cumbersome. It demonstrates some of the more powerful string manipulation facilities in Go, but in real code you'd be much more likely to use something along the lines of the partialStringIterate2.go example.

```
4   func main() {
5     str := "Étoilé"
6     bytes := str[0:7]
7     str2 := string(bytes)
8     for i, c := range str2 {
9       if (0xFFFD == c) {
10        str2 = str2[i:]
11        break
12      } else {
13      fmt.Printf("%c", c)
14      }
15    }
16    fmt.Printf("\n")
17  }
```

From: partialStringIterate2.go

This uses normal string iteration, but checks for the value 0xFFFD, used to represent an invalid rune. If it finds one, then it stores the partial string and then escapes from the loop.

For efficiency, you could skip this check for the majority of the string, and only perform it on the last few bytes. If you find an invalid rune somewhere before the end of the string, it means that your input data is invalid.

This example starts by slicing a string in the middle of a multibyte sequence, in the middle of the trailing é in Étoilé. This is very easy to do by accident. In general, you should avoid slicing strings directly. The utf8 package contains a Slice() function, which slices a string at run indexes, rather than at byte indexes.

Splitting and Trimming Strings

```
2
3   import "strings"
4   import "fmt"
5
6   func main() {
7     str := "\tThis is a string \n"
8     str = strings.Trim(str, " \t\n\r")
9     words := strings.Split(str, " ")
10    for _, word := range words {
11      fmt.Printf("%s\n", word)
12    }
13  }
```

From: trimStrings.go

The *strings package* contains some helpful functions for manipulating string data. This includes splitting and searching strings.

One very common activity is trimming the whitespace from the ends of a string. Both the trimStrings.go and splitString.go examples show ways of doing this.

The first explicitly declares the characters to treat as spaces: space, tab, carriage return, and line feed. The second is more interesting. It uses the `IsSpace()` function from the *unicode package*. This function identifies whether any Unicode character is classed as a space. You can use the same mechanism with other functions to trim other types of leading and trailing data. The unicode package provides some other functions that you can use here, but you can also define your own, to define a set algorithmically.

If you've ever used `strtok()` or `strsep()` in C, then you'll appreciate the ease of splitting strings in Go. The `Split()` function from the strings package splits a string according to a provided separator. In the example at the start of this chapter, we use it to split a string into words, separated by spaces. The result is a slice of strings, so you can easily iterate over it just as you would any other slice.

Splitting a string at a specific character index is a bit harder. The splitString.go example shows what happens when you get this wrong. This shows two ways of splitting a string in half.

```go
package main
import "strings"
import "unicode"
import "exp/utf8string"
import "fmt"

func main() {
    str := "\tthe important rôles of utf8 text\n"
    str = strings.TrimFunc(str, unicode.IsSpace)
    // The wrong way
    fmt.Printf("%s\n", str[0:len(str)/2])
    // The right way
    u8 := utf8string.NewString(str)
    FirstHalf := u8.Slice(0, u8.RuneCount()/2)
    fmt.Printf("%s\n", FirstHalf)
}
```

From: splitString.go

```
the important r?
the important rô
```

Output from: splitString.go

The first way is the obvious approach. You slice
the string, using half its length as the index
for the end of the slice. This, unfortunately,
slices the string right down the center of the ô
character.

The second way is a little bit more involved.
This uses the *exp/utf8string package*, first to
count the number of runes in the string and then
to split the string at a run index, rather than a
byte index.

Note: This example uses a package from the exp hierarchy, which is not part of the standard Go 1.0 install. To run it, you will need to download the exp packages from the Go repository. If you are using the trunk version of Go, you probably have them installed already. Packages in the exp hierarchy are experimental and are intended to become standard parts of the Go library when they are finished. If you are using a Go release after 1.0 then you may find that the package is available without the exp/ prefix.

This involved creating a `String` structure, wrapping the string. If you're doing a lot of complex things to a string, then this is a lot more efficient than using the underlying string directly.

Note that the utf8string package is in the exp hierarchy. This means that it is considered experimental and its functionality may be incorporated into another package (unicode/utf8 would be an obvious choice) or change before the package is finalized.

Copying Strings

```
5   str := "A string"
6   bytes := make([]byte, len(str))
7   copy(bytes, str)
8   strCopy := string(bytes)
```

From: stringCopy.go

Strings in Go are immutable, so there is no need
to copy them. There is, however, a need to copy
the data that they contain. The `copy()` built-
in function allows you to copy a string into a
preallocated byte slice, returning the number of
bytes that it copied.

Once you've got the string data in a slice, you
can modify it in any way that you want. You
can then construct a new string from the slice
with the standard `string()` conversion. You
can also use `append()` to append a string to an
existing slice of `bytes`.

Note that when you do this the string data will
be copied twice, once into the slice and once to
create the new string. This is fairly inefficient, so
it should be avoided except for short strings.

Creating Strings from Patterns

```
5   str := fmt.Sprintf("%T %#v, %d, %v", main, main,
        42, "aubergine")
```

From: sprintf.go

Most of the examples so far have used the `fmt.Printf()` function for output. This is quite similar to the standard C `printf()` function, but with a few improvements. The main difference is due to how Go handles variadic functions. Every argument passed to `Printf()` after the format string is passed in a slice of empty interface elements. The function can inspect each one and see what its type is.

This means that most of the format specifiers in C's `printf()` function are redundant. Their main purpose is to tell the function how to decode arguments that are pushed onto the stack. Go functions don't need help with that.

That's not to say that they're entirely pointless. There is sometimes ambiguity as to how a value should be represented. For example, the `%f` format specifier omits an exponent from floating-point values, while `%E` always displays them.

Go introduces three interesting format specifiers, shown in the example at the start of this section. The `%v` specifier shows the value in its default format, either using a built-in formatter or calling the `String()` method on structures that implement one. The `%#v` specifier is similar, but it outputs the value as a Go-syntax literal value. `%T` prints the type.

The last of these can be incredibly useful for debugging. If you have received a value somewhere in some code via an empty interface, you can just print its type with this function, rather than having to trace all of the way back to where it was declared.

Matching Patterns in Strings

```
5   var static = regexp.MustCompile(", *")
6
7   func main() {
8     r, _ := regexp.Compile("abcd*")
9     str := "abcddd fish, wibble abcd, abc, foo"
10    fmt.Printf("Replaced: %v\n", r.ReplaceAllString
          (str, "bar"))
11    fmt.Printf("Replaced: %v\n", static.
          ReplaceAllString(str, ". "))
12  }
```

From: regex.go

Most modern languages provide some support for regular expressions. Some, like Perl and JavaScript, embed this support in the language. Most others provide them as part of the standard library.

In Go, regular expressions are provided via the *regexp package*. This defines a **Regexp** type, encapsulating a regular expression. These are created by compiling string representations of regular expressions into an internal state-machine representation. The compiled regular expression can then be applied to strings, byte slices, or rune readers.

The example at the start of this section shows

one of the most common uses for regular expressions: replacing all matching occurrences in a string with a new pattern. You can also request the locations of the matches and perform your own substitution, or simply report their locations.

Compiling a regular expression is quite expensive. If you are using a regular expression more than once, then it's a good idea to create it once and then store it. The `MustCompile()` function helps with this. It is equivalent to `Compile()` when the input string is valid, but panics if it is not. If you use it when initializing globals, as in the example, then your program will fail to start if your regular expression is invalid.

7

Working with Collections

Go, in common with most other languages, provides arrays as a fundamental low-level collection type. It adds slices on top of arrays to provide a safe way of accessing arbitrary memory ranges.

In the standard library, Go also provides a small range of collection types, but there's also one more that is part of the language: *maps*. Other languages call these *dictionaries*, *associative arrays*, or (not quite accurately) *hash tables*. They define a unique set of keys, each of which has one value associated with it.

Creating a Map

```go
package main
import "fmt"

type Any interface {}

func main() {
    a := make(map[int] string)
    b := make(map[Any] int)
    a[12] = "A string in a map"
    b[12] = 12
    b["12"] = 13
    b[12.0] = 14
    fmt.Printf("%s %d %d\n", a[12], b[12], b["12"])
}
```

From: map.go

If you've ever worked on a C project, then you've probably implemented some form of map. The lack of any kind of map data type in the standard library is one of the things that people most often miss when moving from a high-level language to C.

The designers of Go decided to add a map as a built-in type to address this. The map type in Go is similar to the **std::map** type in C++. It is defined by the types of its keys and values.

There are no restrictions on the type of the values stored in a map. Keys are a little bit more complicated. Typically, you will want to use either integers or strings as keys in a map. Explicitly stating the type allows the compiler to warn you if you are trying to use the wrong type as a key.

You can also use an interface type as a map key.
This is very flexible, but turns off the compile-
time type checking. The compiler will let you use
any type that implements the interface as a key,
but that doesn't mean that it will work.

Key types must have the equality operator
defined, and there is no operator overloading in
Go, so this restricts you to the built-in types.
This includes pointers, so you can use pointer
types as map keys. Prior to 1.0, using structures
as keys would generate a run-time panic. In Go
1.0, equality is defined on structures recursively,
so two structures are equal if their fields are all
equal.

```
1    A string in a map 12 13
```

Output from: map.go

Note that there is no conversion performed when
you use different types as keys. The example
from the start of this chapter defines a map
from an interface type to integers. It then uses
three different representations of the number 12
(integer, string, and floating-point) as keys. All
of these set different values. This may come as a
surprise if you are used to a language with weak
typing.

Maps, like other Go reference types, are created
with the **make()** built-in function. If you try

to create a map with **new()**, then this will
appear to work, but you will get a pointer to
an uninitialized reference to map, rather than a
reference to a map. The map that this points to
will be the nil map, and any attempt to modify
it will cause a run-time panic. The following
code is valid Go, and so it will compile; it just
won't work:

```
c := new(map[int] string)
// This will panic at run time.
(*c)[1] = "foo"
```

The fact that **new()** returns a pointer while
make() returns a reference makes it difficult
to make this mistake in practice. It's hard to
accidentally type (*c) when you mean c, and if
you wrote c here then the compiler would reject
the code because you're trying to use a pointer
as a map.

The **make()** function takes the map type as the
first argument. If a second argument is specified,
then this is the initial capacity of the map.
Most of the time, you can ignore this. Maps will
dynamically resize themselves as elements are
added. If you are about to add a large (known)
number of entries to a map, then you can avoid
some resizing overhead by creating a map of the
required size initially, but usually it's safe to just
let the map grow as required.

Storing Unordered Groups of Objects

```
1   package main
2   import "fmt"
3
4   func main() {
5     set := make(map[string] bool)
6     set["A"] = true
7     fmt.Printf("%t %t\n", set["A"], set["B"])
8     // Setting to false does not remove the value
9     set["A"] = false
10    for k, v := range set {
11      fmt.Printf("%s %t\n", k, v)
12    }
13    // Remove the element from the set
14    delete(set,"A")
15    for k, v := range set {
16      fmt.Printf("%s %t\n", k, v)
17    }
18  }
```

From: set.go

You can think of a set as a map from objects to boolean values. In Go, that's exactly how you would implement one.

This works because of the idea of a *zero value*, which is essential to a lot of Go patterns. Every Go type has an associated zero value. This is the value that is created by interpreting a block of zero-value bytes that is the same size as the type as an instance of that type.

When you look up a key that is not present in a map, the map returns the zero value. The zero value for a bool is false. You can therefore test membership in a set by simply checking whether the value for a specific key is true or false.

The example from the start of this section defines a set of strings and shows the one slight complication with this approach. A zero value is returned both when the key does not exist and when the key is associated with the zero value. This is apparent when you iterate over the map. The first loop tells you that the key "A" is associated with the value **false**.

You can also explicitly remove values from the map, rather than setting them to the zero value, by using the **delete()** built-in function. This takes a map as the first argument and the key to remove as the second.

Using Lists

```
 6   l := list.New()
 7   l.PushBack(42)
 8   l.PushBack(main)
 9   l.PushBack("A string")
10   for e := l.Back() ; e != nil ; e = e.Prev() {
11     fmt.Printf("%v\n", e.Value)
12   }
```

From: list.go

The Go standard library defines a few collections, including lists. The *list package* contains a good example of how interface types in Go can be composed. Lists are formed from elements, which wrap some other Go type. This means that you can store anything that you want in a list.

Note that, unlike maps, lists are not built in. This means that you only have one list type, not one list type for every possible element type. You can only pass types as arguments to built-in functions like `new()` and `make()`, not to library functions like `list.New()`. So it is impossible to have a list of a specific type without using type introspection, and if you do that then you still don't get compile-time checking.

Lists use the *empty interface type* for objects stored in list entries. We looked at this in Chapter 4, *Common Go Patterns*. It allows any Go type to be stored, without any checking.

In practice, this lack of explicit type checking is rarely a problem. If you really feel that you need it, then you can define some wrappers that set and get list elements with explicit types and always use them.

In the example at the start of this section, we store three differently typed values in a list: an integer, a string, and a function. This shows the type-agnostic nature of the list in particular, and the empty interface type in general.

Defining New Collections

```go
4   type Hashable interface {
5     Hash() int
6     IsEqual(Hashable) bool
7   }
8   type HashTable struct {
9     table map[int] []Hashable
10  }
11  func (h HashTable) Find(value Hashable) Hashable{
12    if (h.table == nil) { return nil }
13    l := h.table[value.Hash()]
14    if l == nil { return nil }
15    for _, e := range(l) {
16      if value.IsEqual(e) {
17        return e
18      }
19    }
20    return nil
21  }
22  func (h *HashTable) Add(value Hashable) {
23    if h.Find(value) != nil { return }
24    hash := value.Hash()
25    if (h.table == nil) {
26      h.table = make(map[int] []Hashable)
27    }
28    l := h.table[hash]
29    h.table[hash] = append(l, value)
30  }
```

From: hashTable.go

If you are designing a new collection, it's usually
a good idea to be as generic as possible. This
means using the empty interface type if you can,
and a simple interface if you can't.

The example at the start of this section shows
a simple hash table implementation, with

secondary chaining. This uses a map from integers to slices and then chains values off the end of each slice. The Go specification does not define how the map is implemented, but in existing implementations it's already a hash table, so this is slightly redundant and would not make much sense outside of an example.

For things to go into a hash table, they must be able to provide a hash, and they must define equality. The `Hashable` interface defines two methods that must be implemented by values going into the hash table.

If you wanted to store some of the Go primitive types in this collection, then you'd have a problem. Something like a `string` or an `int` does not implement these (or any other) methods, so you can't pass one to a function that requires its arguments to do so.

Fortunately, there is a simple solution. You can define a new type that uses one of these as the underlying representation and then add methods to that. The example does this for strings, defining a `str` type that is a string with the required extra methods.

```
32  type str string
33  func (s str) Hash() int {
34    return len(s)
35  }
36  func (s str) IsEqual(other Hashable) bool {
37    return s == other.(str)
38  }
39
40  func main() {
41    var h HashTable
42    h.Add(str("Foo"))
43    h.Add(str("Foo"))
44    h.Add(str("Bar"))
45    h.Add(str("Wibble"))
46    fmt.Printf("%v %v %v\n", h.Find(str("Foo")), h.
          Find(str("Bar")), h.Find(str("Wibble")))
47  }
```

From: hashTable.go

8

Handling Errors

Most code contains bugs. Good code is aware of this and will handle them gracefully. Really good code uses formal methods to prove that there are no bugs, but most people can't afford really good code.

Most of the sample code in this book pretends that errors never happen. This book has quite small pages, and proper error-handling code for any of the examples would fill them up very quickly with things that are largely irrelevant to the point of the example.

Most errors that can be detected at run time come from one function or method calling another with invalid inputs. The best way of handling this depends a lot on the language. For example, Erlang discourages defensive programming at the module level; if your module is in an undefined state, you should kill it and create a new version. In C, you are encouraged to validate every input and check every return

value. In Java, you can defer error handling
by using exceptions. Lisp and Smalltalk let
you inspect the stack when an error occurs
and dynamically fix the code that gave you the
wrong input.

Go doesn't have a one-size-fits-all solution for
errors. There are two common patterns for
errors, depending on their severity, and some
others that can be used for specific situations.

Deferring Cleanup

```
4   func callLocked(lock *sync.Mutex, f func()) {
5     lock.Lock()
6     defer lock.Unlock()
7     f()
8   }
```

From: defer.go

Quite often there's a lot of code between the
place that caused an error and the place that
can handle it. Quite often, it is important for
code to be safe in both the presence and absence
of errors. If your function is somewhere between
a panic and a recover,[1] it should not break.

One obvious example of this is releasing a
mutex. We'll look at mutexes in more detail in
Chapter 9, *Goroutines*. If you've not come across
them before in another language, you can think
of them as simple locks. Once a mutex is locked,

---

[1]Explained in detail in the next section.

any other goroutine attempting to lock it will block until the mutex is unlocked. This means that forgetting to unlock a mutex that you've locked can cause your program to deadlock.

If you acquire a mutex, then you should make sure that you release it no matter how your function exits, whether via an explicit return, implicitly reaching the end of the function, or a panic causing the stack to unwind.

The **defer** statement lets you do exactly this. You can think of this as being analogous to GCC's `__attribute__((cleanup))`, C++ local destructors, or `finally` and `@finally` in Java and Objective-C, respectively. The function call in the **defer** statement happens when the function exits.

The example at the start of this section shows a function that takes a mutex and a function as arguments, and calls the function with the mutex lock. The complete example calls this with a nil function, which causes a runtime panic. No matter what happens when the function is called, this function will then unlock the mutex. Of course, the program may then still abort, but the cleanup code should still run correctly. If the goroutine where this function was called terminates for any reason, it will not accidentally leave the mutex locked.

You can use this same mechanism for releasing operating system resources, for example closing a file that you have been using. This ensures that your code does not leak file descriptors. The garbage collection in Go means that you do not have to use this mechanism to free memory.

Panicking and Recovering

```go
package main
import "fmt"

func badFunction() {
  fmt.Printf("Select Panic type (0=no panic, 1=
      int, 2=runtime panic)\n")
  var choice int
  fmt.Scanf("%d", &choice)
  switch choice {
    case 1:
      panic(0)
    case 2:
      var invalid func()
      invalid()
  }
}

func main() {
  defer func() {
    if x := recover(); x != nil {
      switch x.(type) {
        default: panic(x)
        case int:
            fmt.Printf("Function panicked with a
                very unhelpful error: %d\n", x)
      }
    }
  }()
  badFunction()
  fmt.Printf("Program exited normally\n")
}
```

From: panic.go

You may have heard that Go does not have
exceptions. This is somewhat misleading. Go's
panic mechanism is semantically equivalent to

an exception in other languages. What Go lacks is a culture of using exceptions for flow control.

Exceptions are so named because they are intended to be used for exceptional conditions. A lot of programmers seem to interpret this to mean that they don't happen on quite every call. Go uses the stronger term, panic, to indicate that this mechanism should only be used when there is no obvious recovery mechanism.

The most common response to a panic is for the program to exit. In some cases, it may be possible to recover. In a multiuser program, such as a web app, the correct response to a panic might be to delete the session that caused the panic but not touch any other users' data.

In general, it's much easier to decide when to panic than when to recover. You should panic when you can't think of a good way of continuing. For example, Go will panic if you try to dereference a nil pointer. This implies that something has gone wrong somewhere, and continuing would probably be dangerous.

Deciding when to recover is harder. A panic is usually caused by some very unexpected behavior, so the program may be in an undefined state. Attempting to resume is often a bad idea. Even attempting to clean up can be dangerous: there was a vulnerability in OpenSSH not so long ago that was caused by a bug in cleanup code that ran as the result of abnormal termination.

This mechanism is controlled by the `panic()` and `recover()` built-in functions. The `panic()` function takes an empty interface argument (i.e. a value of any type) and begins unwinding the stack, executing any of the code in any **defer** statements as it goes.

If a **defer** statement contains a call to `recover()`, the argument to `panic()` is returned. This will be `nil` if the **defer** clause is being called as a result of a normal function exit, not as part of a panic.

The example at the start of this section shows two ways of panicking: one with an explicit call to `panic()` and one by calling an invalid function, which causes the runtime to generate a panic.

The **defer** statement uses `recover()` to check for the panic. It then uses a *type switch statement* to determine the type of the panic. If it's an `int`, then we know that it's the example panic and so just discard it. Otherwise, we pass it back to `panic()`. Note the output for the runtime panic shows that it was recovered, before the program exited.

This example has largely used the panic and recover mechanism to implement a try-catch-finally mechanism. The point of this is to show you that the panicking is as expressive as these mechanisms, not to show you good practice. In general, you should avoid calling `recover()` unless you are absolutely certain that it is safe to

```
1   $ ./6.out
2   Select Panic type (0=no panic, 1=int, 2=runtime
        panic)
3   0
4   Program exited normally
5   $ ./6.out
6   Select Panic type (0=no panic, 1=int, 2=runtime
        panic)
7   2
8   panic: runtime error: invalid memory address or
        nil pointer dereference [recovered]
9      panic: runtime error: invalid memory address or
           nil pointer dereference
10
11     [signal 0xb code=0x1 addr=0x0 pc=0x0]
12
13     runtime.panic+0xac /Users/theraven/go/src/pkg/
           runtime/proc.c:1060
14        runtime.panic(0x5e008, 0xf8400013d0)
15
16   $ ./6.out
17   Select Panic type (0=no panic, 1=int, 2=runtime
        panic)
18   1
19   Function panicked with a very unhelpful error: 0
```

Output from: panic.go

recover.

If you are recovering from expected panics, as
happens in this example, then it's a good sign
that your code is wrong. Panics should never be
expected in good code, because it means that
you've missed some error handling. The call to
`invalid` in `badFunction()` should be bracketed
with a check that it is not a nil function.

Returning Error Values

```
1   package main
2   import "errors"
3   import "fmt"
4   import "math"
5
6   func sqrt(i int) (result float64, error error) {
7     if i < 0 {
8       return 0, errors.New("Invalid argument")
9     }
10    return math.Sqrt(float64(i)), nil
11  }
12
13  func main() {
14    // Ignoring error value, because 2 is a valid
          input
15    r, _ := sqrt(2)
16    fmt.Printf("sqrt(2) = %f\nEnter another number\
          n", r)
17    var i int
18    fmt.Scanf("%d", &i)
19    root, err := sqrt(i)
20    if err == nil {
21      fmt.Printf("sqrt(%d) = %f\n", i, root)
22    } else {
23      fmt.Printf("Error: %s\n", err.Error())
24    }
25  }
```

From: error.go

The common way of returning errors in C is to
return a known-invalid value, like -1 or NULL,
and then use a side channel for passing back the
error value. There are two major problems with
this approach. It is not easy to spot code that is
missing error checks and it requires overloading

values, which makes the code hard to read.

In Go, the most common idiom for reporting errors is to use the *multiple return values* capability to return the normal result and an error. It is obvious when code is missing error checking because it is ignoring the error return value.

The example at the start of this section defines a simple `sqrt()` function that returns an error if you pass it a negative input, which would give a complex number as a result and could therefore not be returned as a `float64`.

The first call to this function ignores the error value. Without the comment, someone reading the code would be suspicious of this cavalier disregard for the error code. With the comment, they'd still not regard it as good code, but would understand why it was omitted.

When passing user-provided input to the function, checking the error is important, so in the second call the error is checked and we give up if there is any error.

This function shows the **error** built-in type. This is an interface that just defines one method, for generating a string value describing the error. The simplest way of constructing these is to use the `New()` function, which is currently the only function defined in the *errors package*. This returns a new **error** wrapping a string.

For more complex error reporting, you may want to provide your own structure implementing this interface and providing some extra fields or methods that users can examine for better error handling.

Lots of low-level code uses the **Errno** type, which wraps a UNIX-style error number. Unlike the UNIX or C version, this is returned using the same mechanism that we've just seen, not some side-channel involving macros and thread-local storage.

Error Delegates

```go
5   type sqrtError interface {
6     invalidArgument(int) (int, error)
7   }
8   func sqrt(i int, e sqrtError) (result float64,
          err error) {
9     for i < 0 {
10      var err error
11      i, err = e.invalidArgument(i)
12      if err != nil {
13        return 0, err
14      }
15    }
16    return math.Sqrt(float64(i)), nil
17  }
```

From: errorDelegate.go

One powerful error handling pattern that is not yet common in Go is the *error delegate pattern*. This pattern is well suited to Go's interface typing, which makes it very easy to create simple objects.

Error delegates in Go are interfaces with one method per type of error, implementing a recovery behavior. The example at the start of this section shows the last example, extended to take an error delegate as an argument.

This is a slightly oversimplified example, which contains an obvious bug—it doesn't check that the error delegate is not `nil` before calling `invalidArgument()` on it, so it will crash if you pass `nil` as the error delegate—but it should serve to illustrate the general pattern.

When the error is encountered, rather than aborting, the code now gives the error delegate a chance to fix it—in this case, by providing a replacement for the invalid argument. The exact mechanism by which this replacement is provided is up to the caller.

The errorDelegate.go example includes a simple example delegate that just asks the user for another version. Alternatively, one might just return an absolute value. In extreme cases, it might panic.

This pattern takes a little bit more effort to use than the simple error-value return and so is best used for errors in complex functions. In this example, it is massive overkill, because it's faster and as powerful to simply retry the `sqrt()` call with different arguments if an error is encountered. If a function performs a lot of complex steps and might fail at any point in the middle, then it's better to use something like

```
19   type sqrtHandler struct {}
20   func (_ sqrtHandler) invalidArgument(i int) (int,
         error) {
21     fmt.Printf("%d is not valid, please enter
           another value\n", i)
22     fmt.Scanf("%d", &i)
23     return i, nil
24   }
25
26   func main() {
27     fmt.Printf("Enter a number\n")
28     var i int
29     fmt.Scanf("%d", &i)
30     root, err := sqrt(i, sqrtHandler{})
31     if err == nil {
32       fmt.Printf("sqrt(%d) = %f\n", i, root)
33     } else {
34       fmt.Printf("Error: %s\n", err.Error())
35     }
36   }
```

From: errorDelegate.go

this.

For example, if you had a function that copied
a lot of files, then an error delegate would be a
good way of handling problems. You may want
to continue if one file copy fails, or you may wish
to abort, or possibly modify the file permissions
(or allow the user to do so) and continue.

Goroutines

Goroutines are the basic primitive for concurrency in Go and are very easy to create. Go is intended for a world in which the number of available cores keeps increasing, so it encourages a concurrent programming style. The easy creation of goroutines is a key part of that.

Creating Goroutines

```
6   go fmt.Printf("Printed in the background\n")
7   i := 1
8   go fmt.Printf("Currently, i is %d\n", i)
9   go func() {
10    fmt.Printf("i: %d\n", i)
11  }()
12  i++
13  time.Sleep(1000000000)
```

From: goroutine.go

You create a new goroutine by prefixing any function call with the keyword **go**. This creates a new goroutine containing the call frame and schedules it to run.

The newly created goroutine behaves like a thread in other languages. It can access its arguments, any globals, and anything reachable from them.

If you want to do more than just call an existing function, then you can combine the **go** statement with an anonymous function. The third **go** statement in the example shows a common error in writing this kind of code, as you can see from the output.

```
1  Printed in the background
2  Currently, i is 1
3  i: 2
```

Output from: goroutine.go

The goroutine that references the variable i takes it as a parameter. This means that its value is copied into the call frame for the new goroutine. The second goroutine references it indirectly via the closure. This means that it shares a reference to i with the caller. When the caller increments the variable, the change is reflected in the goroutine.

When I ran this example, the third **Printf()** statement told me that i was 2, but this is not guaranteed. The goroutine may execute immediately, or it may execute before the increment.

The situation is actually slightly more complicated than that. We looked at the Go memory model in Chapter 1, *Introducing Go*. The compiler does not have any constraints on the ordering of memory accesses from a concurrent goroutine, so it is completely free to fold the increment into the initialization. This means that the line written after the goroutine was created may actually run before.

The `Sleep()` call at the end stops the main goroutine from exiting before the spawned one has had a chance to produce any output. Go does not require all goroutines to exit before the program terminates.

Synchronizing Goroutines

```
 1  package main
 2  import "fmt"
 3  import "sync"
 4
 5  func main() {
 6    m := make(map[int] string)
 7    m[2] = "First Value"
 8    var lock sync.Mutex
 9    go func() {
10      lock.Lock()
11      m[2] = "Second Value"
12      lock.Unlock()
13    }()
14    lock.Lock()
15    v := m[2]
16    lock.Unlock()
17    fmt.Printf("%s\n", v)
18  }
```

From: mutex.go

As we saw in the last section, it's often
important to enforce some synchronization
between concurrent parts of the program. This
is not surprising: if some background task is
completely independent of everything else,
then it should probably be part of a different
program.

The *sync package* provides mutexes. These are
simple locks that can be held by at most one
goroutine at a time. Mutexes are an example
of the *zero initialization pattern* that we saw in
Chapter 4, *Common Go Patterns*. This means
that a mutex with a zero value is treated as

an unlocked mutex and is ready to use. The
example at the start of this section shows this:
the mutex is used as soon as it is created, with
no explicit initialization required.

Note: In this chapter, we're looking at some
low-level synchronization primitives that are similar
to the ones that you would expect to find in other
languages. Using things like mutexes and condition
variables is often not good idiomatic Go. You
would often be better served by some of the
techniques covered in Chapter 10, *Concurrency
Design Patterns*.

Mutexes in Go work just as they do in any other
language. They provide two methods, `Lock()`
and `Unlock()`, for acquiring and releasing the
mutex.

The example at the start of this section uses a
mutex to protect a map. Operations on maps
are not atomic, so attempts to modify them
concurrently from two goroutines have undefined
behavior. This example use a simple lock to
protect the map so that the two goroutines can
attempt to modify it without any problems.
We'll look at a better way of implementing
a concurrent map in Go in Chapter 10,
Concurrency Design Patterns.

Note that this approach doesn't make any
guarantees about which order the two goroutines
access the map. Most of the time you run this

example, you will see the first value printed, because the spawned goroutine will not finish starting until after the original has acquired the lock.

It is possible to enforce ordering by moving the `lock.Lock()` line out of the spawned goroutine. The main goroutine will then block on the second `lock.Lock()` call until the spawned goroutine releases the lock by calling `lock.Unlock()` before returning.

This means that Go "mutexes" are actually *binary semaphores*, rather than true mutexes. They do not have an owner, which means that they cannot support recursive use (calling `Lock()` on the same mutex twice in the same goroutine causes it to deadlock) and that they do not support error checking behavior. These would be very irritating limitations in other languages.

Waiting for a Condition

```
 1  package main
 2  import "fmt"
 3  import "sync"
 4
 5  func main() {
 6    m := make(map[int] string)
 7    m[2] = "First Value"
 8    var mutex sync.Mutex
 9    cv := sync.NewCond(&mutex)
10    updateCompleted := false
11    go func() {
12      cv.L.Lock()
13      m[2] = "Second Value"
14      updateCompleted = true
15      cv.Signal()
16      cv.L.Unlock()
17    }()
18    cv.L.Lock()
19    for !updateCompleted {
20      cv.Wait()
21    }
22    v := m[2]
23    cv.L.Unlock()
24    fmt.Printf("%s\n", v)
25  }
```

From: condvar.go

Go provides condition variables, which are
similar to their POSIX equivalent. The
condvar.go example extends the example from
the last section to ensure that the write from
the concurrent goroutine has completed before
reading. For this simple use, it would be better
to use a wait group, as discussed in the section

Performing Actions in the Background.

A condition variable allows one or more goroutines to sleep until some condition is met. They are typically used in a solution to the *producer-consumer problem*. It's quite unlikely that you will actually want to use them in Go, because channels provide a much better solution to this, but they can be useful when implementing algorithms designed for other systems.

Condition variables have a lock associated with them. The Go implementation allows any type that implements the **Locker** interface to be used, but in this example we use a mutex. The **L** field of the condition variable can be used to access this lock directly.

When you call **Wait()**, the lock is atomically released and the goroutine goes to sleep. If the lock is not held by the calling goroutine, then the call to **Wait()** will panic. When another goroutine calls either **Signal()** or **Broadcast()** on the condition variable, then sleeping goroutines wake up and attempt to reacquire the lock. **Signal()** wakes just one, while **Broadcast()** wakes them all.

Typically, you will want to call these functions with the lock held, or there is a chance of wakeup events being lost. This is not required and can be avoided if you know that they will be called later with the lock held.

Condition variables, as their name would imply,

are intended to be used to monitor a condition. In this example, the condition that the `cv` condition variable is protecting is the state of the `updateCompleted` variable. If this variable is true, then we say that the condition holds. Conditions do not have to be simple variables; they can also be the result of some computation.

The example shows the common pattern for using a condition variable. The producer acquires the lock, updates the condition (the `updateCompleted` variable), and then signals the condition variable (`cv`) before releasing the lock. The consumer acquires the lock, tests the condition, and, if it doesn't hold, then it sleeps on the condition variable. It then reacquires the lock when the producer releases it, releases it itself, and continues.

There are two possible execution orders for this example. The original goroutine—the `main()` function—may acquire the lock first. If this happens, then `updateCompleted` will be `false`, so it will call `Wait()`, atomically releasing the lock. At this point, the spawned goroutine will acquire the lock, do its modifications, and then signal the condition variable and release the lock, allowing the original goroutine to continue.

Alternatively, the spawned goroutine will grab the lock first. In this case, the original goroutine will probably block on the `Lock()` call, although it may not if the spawned goroutine completes its updates first. Either way, it will not proceed past this line until the other goroutine has released the lock. At this point, `updateCompleted` will be `true`, so it won't wait and will proceed to completion immediately.

Performing Thread-Safe Initialization

```go
type LazyInit struct {
  once sync.Once
  value int
}
func (s *LazyInit) Value() int {
  s.init()
  return s.value
}
func (s *LazyInit) init() {
  s.once.Do(func() { s.value = 42 })
}
func (s *LazyInit) SetValue(v int) {
  s.value = v
}

func main() {
  var l LazyInit
  fmt.Printf("%d\n", l.Value())
  l.SetValue(12)
  fmt.Printf("%d\n", l.Value())
}
```

From: once.go

Most Go structures use the zero initialization pattern, so when you create a structure that uses them, you generally don't do explicit initialization. Sometimes, however, you do,

and it's often best to support *lazy initialization*
rather than require an explicit call to an
initializer.

The example from the start of this section shows
a trivial type that encapsulates an integer. This
supports the zero initialization pattern, but it
has an initial value of 42, rather than zero. To
support this, it uses the `Once` type from the sync
package. This is similar to `pthread_once()` in
the POSIX threading API, although it's easier to
use.

The `Once` object has a `Do()` method, which
takes a function as an argument. It will run that
function exactly once, as you might have guessed
from the name. This is thread-safe, so calling
`Do()` twice from different goroutines will still
only run it once, and will cause the second caller
to block until the first has completed.

In general, this pattern will be more expensive
than using a designated initializer. At best, it
will require one extra branch to check whether
the object has been initialized. A good Go
compiler will make this overhead small, but it
will still exist.

Performing Actions in the Background

```go
func main() {
  var w sync.WaitGroup
  for _, v := range os.Args {
    w.Add(1)
    go func(str string) {
      fmt.Printf("%s\n", strings.ToUpper(str))
      w.Done()
    }(v)
  }
  w.Wait()
}
```

From: wait.go

Performing some action in the background is one of the most common uses for a goroutine. If you have all of the data required for a calculation, but you don't need the result immediately, then you can start it running in the background in a goroutine and then do something else and wait for it to complete when you actually need the result.

The *sync package* provides *wait groups* to make this easier. You can implement these yourself with channels quite easily but it's convenient to use the preprepared version. If you're coming from Java, then you may have used the **CountDownLatch** class: Go wait groups are used for a similar purpose.

Wait groups are similar to counting semaphores.

You can increment and decrement their value, and block if the value is not zero. There are two typical ways of using wait groups. In both cases, you call **Done()** from within the background goroutine to indicate that it's finished, but you initialize the waiting value in one of two ways.

If you are launching a fixed-number of background goroutines, then you can just call **Add()** once with the number as the argument. Alternatively, you may be launching a variable number of them. For example, if you are reading input from a channel, then you might want to create a background goroutine for each message that you receive. At the end, you'd want to make sure that you wait for all of the processing to complete.

The example at the start of this section shows how to use wait groups to implement the latter pattern. This iterates over every argument passed to the program and, in the background, prints the uppercase version of it. If you try removing the last line of this example, you'll find that it doesn't print any output: the **main()** function—and therefore the program—exits before the first background goroutine has a chance to print any output.

Using the arguments array here is a fairly trivial example, but it shows how you can spawn an arbitrary number of goroutines in the background and wait for them all to finish.

Communicating Via Channels

```go
package main
import "fmt"

func main() {
  m := make(map[int] string)
  m[2] = "First Value"
  c := make(chan bool, 1)
  go func() {
    m[2] = "Second Value"
    c <- true
  }()
  _ = <- c
  fmt.Printf("%s\n", m[2])
}
```

From: chan.go

Creating parallel subprograms cheaply is useful, but the real strength of Go comes from the ease with which these detached goroutines can communicate. So far this chapter has looked at the primitive synchronization operations that you'd expect to find in any vaguely modern language. Hopefully, you will never need to use these in Go programs.

Go provides *channels*, based on Hoare's *Communicating Sequential Processes* (*CSP*) formalism. A channel is quite like a UNIX pipe: you can put data down one end and get it out at the other. It supports buffering, with a configurable buffer size. Unlike pipes, channels are typed. When you create a channel, you specify the type of values that will be passed along it. Of course, you can use the empty interface type if you want to be able to pass values of any type and detect the type at the receiving end.

Channels encourage a style of programming that scales easily without increasing debugging complexity. All of the techniques that we'll look at in Chapter 10, *Concurrency Design Patterns*, involve channels. Many of them can be implemented in other languages using mutexes, condition variables, and so on, but most of the time this involves implementing channels on top of these lower-level primitives.

You can also replace the lower-level synchronization primitives with channels. The example at the start of this section shows how to replace explicit synchronization via condition variables with implicit synchronization via a channel. This example is equivalent to the one from the last section, but is much simpler.

Note: Most of the examples in this chapter are doing a very small amount of work in a spawned goroutine. It is almost certainly more expensive to set up the synchronization primitives and spawn the concurrent goroutine than it would be to just do the work in the caller. The point of these examples is to demonstrate the use of synchronization mechanisms, not to encourage you to do trivial amounts of work in parallel.

This example starts by creating a channel. As

with maps and slices, channels are created with
the `make()` built-in function. The first argument
is a channel type, and the second is the size
of the buffer. In this example, we just want a
single element buffered, because we're only ever
sending one value over the channel. We use `bool`
as the type for the channel, although any type
would be fine because we're not actually using
the result.

In the spawned goroutine, we send the value
`true` through the channel. The caller tries to
read a value from the channel. This will block
until a value is sent. In this simple example,
we're just discarding the received value.

For clarity, I've assigned the value that we read
from the channel to the blank identifier. In Go,
receive operations are expressions. The `<- c`
part evaluates to the first value received on
channel `c`. This can be either stored somewhere,
passed as a function argument, or ignored. You
can, for example, write `someFunction(<-c)` to
block until a value is received on the channel and
then call `someFunction()` with this value as the
argument.

This is about the simplest possible use for a
channel. It serves to illustrate the fact that
channels provide simple solutions to some of the
problems that you'd typically solve with mutexes
or condition variables in other languages.

Channels are not just a replacement for
condition variables; they allow a flexible

message-passing design for concurrent programs. We'll look at several more complex examples of their use in the rest of the book.

If you're coming from Erlang, then you may find this construct quite familiar. There are some important differences. Erlang uses actor-model concurrency but uses CSP-derived syntax for sending and receiving messages. Go uses CSP, but with its own syntax. The important difference between Erlang's Actor model and CSP is the existence of channels. In Erlang, you send messages to process identifiers. In Go, you send them to channels, which are a slightly higher level of abstraction.

A message sent to a Go channel may be received by any goroutine, including the one that originally sent it. Two messages sent to a single channel may be handled by different goroutines. In contrast, a message sent to an Erlang process is always handled by that process. It's trivial to implement either of these models on top of the other. You can implement Erlang-style communication by simply creating a channel for each goroutine that you spawn and sharing the sending end but keeping the receiving end private. You can implement channels in Erlang by either using an indirection layer, where one process forwards messages to one or more others, or by tagging messages that you send with a channel identifier to allow them to be sorted at the final receiving end.

Using Multiple Channels

```go
func main() {
  abort := make(chan bool)
  count := make(chan int)
  go cancel(abort)
  go countDown(count)
  for {
    select {
      case i := <- count:
        if 0 == i {
          selfDestruct()
          return
        }
        fmt.Printf("%d seconds remaining\n", i)
      case a := <- abort:
        if a {
          fmt.Printf("Self destruct aborted\n")
        } else {
          selfDestruct()
        }
        return
    }
  }
}
```

From: *selfDestruct.go*

Quite often, you want to be able to receive input from one of a small group of goroutines. This is not possible with the normal receive statement, because it blocks when attempting to read from the channel.

The **select** statement is similar to a **switch** statement, but it selects based on the availability of communication channels rather than on a truth value. The **select** statement will pick one

and perform the relevant communication, which
can be a send or a receive operation.

You can also implement a non-blocking receive
with the **select** statement. If there is a
default: clause, then that will be executed
if none of the channels in case statements are
ready; otherwise it will block until one becomes
ready.

```
5   func cancel(abort chan bool) {
6     fmt.Printf("This program will self destruct, do
              you wish to cancel?\n")
7     var r int
8     fmt.Scanf("%c", &r)
9     switch r {
10      default: abort <- false
11      case 'y': abort <- true
12      case 'Y': abort <- true
13    }
14  }
15
16  func countDown(count chan int) {
17    for i := 10 ; i >= 0 ; i-- {
18      count <- i
19      time.Sleep(1000000000)
20    }
21  }
```

From: selfDestruct.go

The selfDestruct.go example uses a **select**
statement to receive input from one of two
channels. One counts down from ten to zero,
once per second, while the other sends a boolean
value based on user input. If the timer reaches

zero, or the user actively chooses not to cancel, then this example calls the `selfDestruct()` function. If the user cancels, then it exits normally.

This same pattern can be employed in any situation where you have multiple possible inputs from channels but don't know which one is likely to have data first. In this example, one channel comes from the user, so it may contain data immediately, never, or some time between the two. Channels from the network also fall into this category.

A more interesting case for this pattern is when you have steps of a parallel computation taking different amounts of time. It lets you receive partial responses in the order in which they are ready and then start the next phase of computation immediately.

Concurrency Design Patterns

In Chapter 9, *Goroutines*, we looked at a number of ways of synchronizing activities between goroutines, using patterns that are common in other languages. As with other facets of the language, there are some idioms that are natural in Go, but which would not make sense in another language.

Concurrency is a core part of Go. Spawning a new goroutine, which is roughly analogous to a thread, requires you to type three characters, including the space. The implementation of these goroutines in gc is similarly lightweight— slightly more than a function call but not much. In gccgo, it is equivalent to an operating system thread.

In the last chapter, we saw that Go has more or less the same set of synchronization primitives as the POSIX threads API. This means that you can take any algorithm designed for threads and implement it in Go very easily. Doing so is usually a bad idea, and is very rarely idiomatic Go. In this chapter, we'll look at some of the techniques for designing scalable applications in Go.

Timing Out Connections

```
12   func timeout(t chan bool) {
13     time.Sleep(5000000000)
14     t <- true
15   }
16
17   func main() {
18     t := make(chan bool)
19     s := make(chan string)
20     go readString(s)
21     go timeout(t)
22     select {
23       case msg := <- s:
24         fmt.Printf("Received: %s\n", msg)
25       case <- t:
26         fmt.Printf("Timed out\n")
27     }
28   }
```

From: timeout.go

Go channels do not support a timeout automatically. This is intentional, because it's difficult to design a timeout mechanism that is sufficiently general to be usable in all situations. Instead, Go provides a mechanism for you to implement timeouts yourself.

The **select** statement allows you to wait for
data from any channel. The example at the
start of this section shows how to spawn a new
goroutine to provide a timeout. This goroutine
sleeps for five seconds and then sends a message
back. The message itself is irrelevant. Here, we
just use a boolean value, but it's only the fact
that the message is sent that matters, not its
content.

The **select** statement here is used to time out
a single connection. Either the first channel
delivers a string within five seconds, or the
timeout will cause anything that it sends to be
ignored.

Note that we don't close the channel that
readString() will write to when the timeout
occurs. If the readString() goroutine put a
string into the channel in between closing it and
exiting, then we'd get a runtime panic, which is
not what we want. Instead, we silently discard
the message that it sends.

That is not always the correct decision. If you
want the other end to be able to know that an
object has been freed, then it's a good idea to
close the channel. This allows the sender to
handle the panic and clean up any resources
related to generating the data. An even better
solution would be to send a canceled message
down another channel, so the goroutine knew
that you'd get bored with waiting for it to finish.

In this example, we're only timing out a single

connection, but this same pattern works for an arbitrary number of channels in the **select** statement. You can implement the timeout signal more efficiently using a timer, as discussed in Chapter 11, *Dates and Times*.

Aliased xor Mutable

There is one rule that makes writing concurrent programs easy:

No object should be both aliased and mutable.

This is a general pattern for any language, but is particularly relevant to Go. Because Go uses a shared-everything model, you can pass pointers to objects down channels easily. You then have two concurrent goroutines that have references to the same object. If you haven't been very careful, you now probably have some race conditions. If you've been slightly careful, you probably have the potential for deadlock.

If two goroutines try to modify the same object simultaneously, then you need to think very carefully about their possible interactions. As any experienced programmer knows, code that you need to think about carefully in order to be sure it is correct is most likely to be code that contains bugs.

To avoid this, follow a simple rule. If you ever pass a pointer through a channel, make sure that you immediately discard your copy of it.

Passing a pointer through a channel should pass ownership of the pointee to the receiver.

The same rule applies to arguments passed when starting a new goroutine. The caller should not keep pointers to any objects that the new goroutine can modify.

You can use slices to enforce this when sharing an array between multiple goroutines. One fairly common use for parallelism is performing the same transformation on every element in an array. You can do this with a collection of goroutines, each working on a small range within the array. If you start each goroutine with a non-overlapping slice of the array, then the array as a whole is only mutable from the calling goroutine. If it then waits for all modifications to complete, then your code is safe. It is not possible to expand a slice beyond its declared capacity, even if the underlying array has enough space to do so.

Share Memory by Communicating

```
 5   type request struct {
 6     key int
 7     value string
 8     ret chan string
 9   }
10
11   func set(m chan request, key int, value string)
         string {
12     result := make(chan string)
13     m <- request{key, value, result}
14     return <-result
15   }
16
17   func runMap(c chan request) {
18     m := make(map[int] string)
19     for {
20       req := <- c
21       old := m[req.key]
22       m[req.key] = req.value
23       req.ret <- old
24     }
25   }
26
27   func main() {
28     m := make(chan request)
29     go runMap(m)
30     fmt.Printf("Set %s\n", set(m, 1, "foo"))
31     fmt.Printf("Set %s\n", set(m, 1, "bar"))
32   }
```

From: sharedMap.go

Channel references are the primary exception to the rule from the last section. It is perfectly safe to share channel references between goroutines, because they provide implicit synchronization.

In a language like C or Java, you would typically implement a shared dictionary by creating a non-concurrent dictionary and a mutex lock. Whenever you wanted to manipulate the dictionary, you would acquire the lock, perform the manipulation, and then release the lock.

This pattern is possible in Go. The *sync package* provides a mutex implementation that can be used for this kind of task. This lets you enjoy all of the difficulties of lock-based programming that you've probably encountered in other languages.

If you are feeling lazy, and would prefer to spend your time worrying about the problems that your program is intended to solve, rather than about the minutiae of thread safety, then Go provides another alternative. The example at the start of this section provides a (very) simple implementation of a shared map. This uses channels for implicit synchronization.

This simple implementation only defines one operation, implemented in the `set()` function, which sets a new value and returns the old one.

The map itself is local to a goroutine. In a cleaner implementation, you would probably put the channel in an opaque interface and have a function that created the goroutine and the channel, rather than exposing the implementation details like this.

When you call the `set()` function, it creates a request, sends it across the channel, and then waits for the reply. The channel performs implicit synchronization for you. Requests sent across the channel are serialized, so there is no possibility of multiple concurrent accesses.

If you extend this map to have separate methods for setting and accessing values, then you can even benefit from concurrency. A set operation does not need to wait for a reply: it can simply push the key and value into the channel and return immediately. This set operation will complete after any pending operations in the queue.

From the perspective of the calling goroutine, any sequence of set and get operations will appear to be processed in sequence. If you do two set operations followed by a get, then only the get will block, and it won't return until after the two set operations have completed. It is completely safe to access the map from multiple goroutines in this way, although you must take care if you want to ensure that updates from one goroutine are seen by another.

Transactions by Sharing Channels

```
36   func HandleRequests(m map[int] string,
37                        c chan Request) {
38     for {
39       req := <- c
40       switch (req.requestType) {
41         case Get:
42           req.ret <- m[req.key]
43         case Set:
44           m[req.key] = req.value
45         case BeginTransaction:
46           HandleRequests(m, req.transaction)
47         case EndTransaction:
48           return
49       }
50     }
51   }
```

From: transactionMap.go

One of the biggest problems with lock-based concurrency is that it is impossible to compose operations in a general way. Imagine that you have a thread-safe map implementation, with set and get operations that can be called from multiple threads and are guaranteed to be atomic. Now try to define an atomic increment operation in terms of these: It's not possible.

An atomic increment operation needs to do a get, and then a modify, and then a set and needs to ensure that there are no other get or set operations happening until it completes. The simplest solution would be to add the atomic increment operation directly to the map and ensure that it holds the same lock that protects the get and set. When you need a more complex composite operation, then you need to further complicate your concurrent map.

This is difficult to get right. Fortunately, Go provides a much simpler mechanism. The transactionMap.go example shows an extended version of the concurrent map from the example in the last section. This version defines operations to begin and end transactions.

Note: The sharedMap.go and transactionMap.go examples both use a structure for sending requests. In the second example, most of the requests only use some of the structure fields. This is not a significant overhead for a simple map, because the request structure is small, so you're only wasting a few bytes if you only use half of it.

For more complex data structures, you may want to consider using an interface type for requests. The interface would define an accessor to get the type, and an accessor to get specific request types. Each structure that implemented the interface would return either itself or nil from each accessor.

If you encapsulate your concurrent data type behind a small set of public functions, then it's very easy to switch between the two approaches.

When you begin a transaction, the goroutine
handling the map temporarily puts the channel
to one side and starts listening for operations
from the new one. This effectively gives the
caller exclusive access to the map for a sequence
of operations, until the transaction has been
completed.

```
19   func get(m chan Request, key int) string {
20     result := make(chan string)
21     m <- Request{Get, key, "", result, nil}
22     return <-result
23   }
24   func set(m chan Request, key int, value string) {
25     m <- Request{Set, key, value, nil, nil}
26   }
27   func beginTransaction(m chan Request) chan
         Request{
28     t := make(chan Request)
29     m <- Request{BeginTransaction, 0, "", nil, t}
30     return t
31   }
32   func endTransaction(m chan Request) {
33     m <- Request{EndTransaction, 0, "", nil, nil}
34   }
```

From: transactionMap.go

With this simple interface to the shared
map, you can trivially implement an atomic
append or atomic capitalize operation on the
values held in the map. You just need to call
`beginTransaction()`, then `get()`, perform
whatever modification you wanted to make, and
finally call `set()` and `endTransaction()`.

This is a fairly primitive implementation of
transactions. These transactions are blocking,
and don't support any form of rollback. A more
complex implementation might create a new
goroutine that handled all of the operations
in the transaction on a copy of the map, and
then passed the set of changes to the original.
This would either merge them or reject them,
depending on whether there were any conflicts.

Concurrent Objects

```
10   type ConcurrentMap struct {
11     ch chan request
12     init sync.Once
13   }
14   func (cm *ConcurrentMap) Set(key int, value
          string) string {
15     cm.init.Do(func () {
16             cm.ch = make(chan request)
17             go runMap(cm.ch)
18             })
19     result := make(chan string)
20     cm.ch <- request{key, value, result}
21     return <-result
22   }
```

From: concurrentMap.go

It's often convenient to use concurrency
implicitly in Go. We've seen how to do that
using some wrapper functions earlier in this
chapter, but these still made the channel
explicit.

The example at the start of this section is a tidier version of the shared map from earlier. If you put this in a package, then users can use the Set() method without ever being aware of the way it is implemented. All that they know is that this is a shared map that can be used safely from multiple goroutines.

This pattern is very useful for testing, because it provides the same benefits as data hiding in other contexts. You can easily change the implementation of the concurrent map. You may want to implement another version using a simple mutex and compare the performance; being able to do this without modifying any code that uses the map is very useful.

The other advantage of using a structure, rather than a collection of functions, is that it lets you use interfaces. You could define a concurrent map and a non-shared map with the same interface, and code that didn't care about thread safety could just use whichever one it was passed.

Implementing Futures in Go

```go
type futureInt64 struct {
  ch chan int64
  v int64
  collect sync.Once
}
func (f *futureInt64) String() string {
  f.collect.Do(func() { f.v = <- f.ch })
  return strconv.FormatInt(f.v, 10)
}
func fib(n int64) (int64, int64) {
  if n < 2 { return 1,1 }
  f1, f2 := fib(n-1)
  return f2, f1+f2
}
func Fib(n int64) fmt.Stringer {
  var ch futureInt64
  ch.ch = make(chan int64)
  go func() {
    _, f := fib(n)
    ch.ch <- f
  }()
  return &ch
}
func main() {
  f := Fib(100)
  fmt.Printf("The 100th Fibonacci number is: ")
  fmt.Printf("%v\n", f)
}
```

From: futureFib.go

With goroutines, you can implement functions
that run in the background. With channels, you
can also collect their results asynchronously. The
pattern shown at the start of this section shows
how to implement *futures*, sometimes called

promises, in Go.

The `Fib()` function computes a number in the Fibonacci sequence, in a newly spawned goroutine, and returns a structure that implicitly synchronizes when it is accessed.

This simple return value only implements one method, declared in the *fmt package*, which converts a value to a string. For more complex return types, you'd need to create a more complex future type, which forwarded all of the declared messages to a field containing the real return value, once it had been received.

The advantage of this approach is that it allows a completely serial programming style, while still providing concurrency. Users of the `Fib()` function may act as if it is a purely sequential function, yet it will run in the background and only actually block the calling goroutine when it tries to use the return value.

As before, the amount of work done in the spawned goroutine is not really enough to justify creating a new goroutine. This pattern is more applicable where you have a bit more work to do.

Coalescing Events

```go
 6  func later(deferRunning chan bool, delay time.
        Duration, f func()) {
 7    t := time.NewTimer(delay)
 8    for {
 9      select {
10        case cont := <- deferRunning:
11          if cont {
12            t = time.NewTimer(delay)
13          } else {
14            f()
15            return
16          }
17        case <- t.C:
18          f()
19          t = time.NewTimer(delay)
20      }
21    }
22  }
23
24  func main() {
25    deferRunning := make(chan bool)
26    buffer := ""
27    go later(deferRunning, 3000000000,
28        func() { fmt.Printf("User entered %s\n",
                buffer) })
29    b := make([]byte, 1)
30    for b[0] != '\n' {
31      os.Stdin.Read(b)
32      deferRunning <- true
33      buffer += string(b)
34    }
35    deferRunning <- false
```

From: idle.go

A common problem in interactive applications is running some code in the background in response to user input without increasing latency. For example, a text editor may want to run a spell checker or syntax highlighting task in the background. In theory, you want to do this after every keystroke, but if you spell check an entire document after every keystroke then you're going to end up doing a lot of redundant work. A better solution, which is almost indistinguishable from the user's perspective, is to run the background task after a few seconds (or a large fraction of a second) of inactivity.

The example at the start of this section shows how to do this. The program first spawns a background goroutine with a function to run when a timeout expires, a channel for deferring it, and a timeout. The function will be called a fixed delay after the last time it is deferred.

Note: Most UNIX systems implement buffering in the terminal. If you run this example from such a terminal then the program will not receive the input until you press Enter, so it will not defer execution of the background task.

This trivial example reads from the standard input, and defers execution of the background task until after it is completed. The task itself is also trivial, but you could easily replace it with something that did real work on the input.

Map Reduce, Go Style

```go
17  func Map(fileName string, intermediate chan
          Partial) {
18    file, err := os.Open(fileName)
19    if err == nil {
20      var s scanner.Scanner
21      s.Init(file)
22      tok := s.Scan()
23      for tok != scanner.EOF {
24        intermediate <- Partial{s.TokenText(),
                fileName}
25        tok = s.Scan()
26      }
27    }
28    intermediate <- Partial{"", ""}
29  }
30
31  func Reduce(token string, files []string, final
          chan Result) {
32    counts := make(map[string] int)
33    for _, file := range files {
34      counts[file]++
35    }
36    final <- Result{token, counts}
37  }
```

From: mapReduce.go

It seems fitting that a programming language developed by Google should make it easy to implement the concurrency pattern that made Google so successful: *Map Reduce*. This involves splitting an algorithm into two concurrent steps. One runs on chunks of the input and produces pairs of intermediate results; the other folds the intermediate results to produce a final result.

The code at the start of this section shows the Go implementations of these two components for the canonical application of Map Reduce: indexing a set of files. In this case, it's creating an index of the tokens used in the examples in this book. The map phase works on a single source file and generates a stream of (filename, token) pairs, which it then delivers as intermediate results.

Once the map phase has run, the reduce phase runs once for each token and counts the number of occurrences of the filename in the generated intermediate lists, providing a final result. You could use this to quickly search these source files: for each search term, you end up with a list of files and the number of times it occurs in that file.

The map and reduce functions are specific to the application of this pattern, but they need to be supported by some more generic code. In this example, the `collectIntermediates()` function does most of this work. This first collects the results from the `Map()` function and then spawns instances of the `Reduce()` function and finally delivers their collected results.

The `collectIntermediates()` function is quite simple. Hopefully you can follow it quite easily: it doesn't contain anything that we haven't looked at already, although it does combine quite a lot of parts of Go in one place. The `Map()` function will send some unknown number of

```go
39  func collectPartials(intermediate chan Partial,
40                       count int,
41                       final chan map[string]
                              map[string] int) {
42    intermediates := make(map[string] []string)
43    for count > 0 {
44      res := <- intermediate
45      if res.value == "" && res.key == "" {
46        count--
47      } else {
48        v := intermediates[res.key]
49        if v == nil {
50          v = make([]string, 0, 10)
51        }
52        v = append(v, res.value)
53        intermediates[res.key] = v
54      }
55    }
56    collect := make(chan Result)
57    for token, files := range intermediates {
58      go Reduce(token, files, collect)
59    }
60    results := make(map[string] map[string] int)
61    // Collect one result for each goroutine we
          spawned
62    for _, _ = range intermediates {
63      r := <- collect
64      results[r.token] = r.counts
65    }
66    final <- results
67  }
```

From: mapReduce.go

intermediate results as it runs. We use an empty
pair as a placeholder indicating that it's finished.
The collectIntermediates() function is called

with a known number of `Map()` goroutines, so it
just decrements this count each time one finishes
and then stops waiting for new results once it
hits zero.

This part of the code builds a list of
intermediate results for each token. When there
are no more partial results to collect, it spawns a
goroutine for each token to do the reduce step.
This then passes back a map containing the
number of times each word appears in a list.
You could produce a better index by putting this
into an array and sorting it by occurrences. I
didn't do that here, because it adds complexity
without showing you any more that's relevant to
implementing the Map Reduce pattern.

After all of the reduce steps have run, this
function again collects their results in a map and
delivers it as the final result. This function is the
only bit of serial code in this pattern; the map
and reduce steps can run with a large degree of
parallelism. As long as the work that they are
doing is large in comparison with collecting the
results, this approach can scale very well.

The program using this is quite simple. The
`main()` function just spawns one copy of the
`Map()` function for each .go file and one copy of
the `collectIntermediates()` function, joins
them with channels, and waits for the result.

Most of the `main()` function is simply
determining whether a file has a .go suffix, and
then printing the final results. As with most

```
69  func main() {
70    intermediate := make(chan Partial)
71    final := make(chan map[string] map[string] int)
72    dir, _ := os.Open(".")
73    names, _ := dir.Readdirnames(-1)
74    go collectPartials(intermediate, len(names),
          final)
75    for _, file := range names {
76      if (strings.HasSuffix(file, ".go")) {
77        go Map(file, intermediate)
78      } else {
79        intermediate <- Partial{"", ""}
80      }
81    }
82    result := <- final
83    for token, counts := range result {
84      fmt.Printf("\n\nToken: %v\n", token)
85      total := 0
86      for file, count := range counts {
87        fmt.Printf("\t%s:%d\n", file, count)
88        total += count
89      }
90      fmt.Printf("Total: %d\n", total)
91    }
92  }
```

From: mapReduce.go

other things we've seen, the indexing step runs
entirely in the background. This version just
blocks waiting for the result to arrive on the
final channel. It's processing a relatively small
amount of data, so will complete in a fraction of
a second. If you passed it a larger input, then
you could do something else while waiting for
the background indexing to complete. This is a

common pattern in API documentation or help viewers: they allow browsing while constructing the index.

As with other Go patterns, there is no explicit synchronization in this example. We don't even import the *sync package*: there are no mutexes, no condition variables, no wait groups. Synchronization happens implicitly via channels. In most Map Reduce implementations, the framework goes to a lot of effort to avoid spawning too many threads to run efficiently. The cheap concurrency in Go means that we don't need to worry about that: we can just spawn a lot of goroutines and let the runtime sort it out.

11

Dates and Times

Unsurprisingly, given its antecedents, Go inherits the UNIX notion of time. Time is represented at the low level by the number of seconds since the UNIX Epoch: the start of 1970 UTC. Local time is calculated from this by applying a time zone offset, and can then be converted into something suitable for display, such as a year, month, and day.

Most Go APIs use nanoseconds for *time intervals*. It's important to differentiate between time and time intervals. A time is a fixed point relative to some epoc date and depends on things like the current time zone. A time interval, in contrast, is a quantity that makes sense in isolation.

The *time package* includes two types for representing these two concepts. A `Duration` represents a length of time, while a `Time` represents a fixed point in time.

Finding the Current Date

```
7    fmt.Printf("%d seconds since the Epoc\n", now.
         Unix())
8    fmt.Printf("%d nanoseconds since the Epoc\n", now
         .UnixNano())
```

From: now.go

The lowest-level mechanism for getting the time is in the *runtime package* and is private to the implementation. The private **now()** function in the runtime is a very thin wrapper around the **gettimeofday()** system call on UNIX and its equivalent on other systems. The system call returns a structure containing the number of elapsed seconds and microseconds.

The *time package* provides a convenient function, **Now()**, which returns a **Time** structure encapsulating the time. This structure also contains a time zone, so you can safely compare instances of it even if they are related to different events. You can then use its **Unix()** and **UnixNano()** methods, which return the time in seconds and nanoseconds, respectively.

The **Time** structure provides a large number of other methods for inspecting and comparing times. We'll look at some of them in the rest of this chapter.

Converting Dates for Display

```
7   now := time.Now()
8   fmt.Printf("Today is %s\n", now.Format("Monday"))
9   fmt.Printf("The time is %s\n", now.Format(time.
        Kitchen))
```

From: localNow.go

When it comes to user interaction, we unfortunately see some big gaps in the Go standard library. Just as C assumed that everyone used text representable in ASCII, Go assumes that everyone uses the Gregorian calendar. This is fine if you only expect to have users in America or Europe, but in other parts of the world it's likely to cause problems.

Note: Check the current documentation for the time package before using it. Hopefully it will have improved by the time you read this. The current implementation is full of implicit US-centric conventions. It is difficult to use in code that needs to work in Europe (it does not allow non-English day names to be used in format strings), and impossible to use in countries using the Islamic or Chinese calendars, which are completely unsupported.

If you only have to worry about people using the Gregorian calendar, then Go provides some useful features. The **Time** structure encapsulates a local date, as represented by the Gregorian calendar. This has public fields containing things like the month and day. You can either access these fields explicitly, or you can use the `Format()` method to prepare such a date for display.

Go date format strings are slightly non-obvious. Rather than defining a format string with escape sequences for things like the day of the week, they uses a specific date. This date is the fifth second after the fourth minute of the third hour in the afternoon of the second day of the first month, in the sixth year in the second millennium, with time zone offset -0700. This date was chosen because the value for each date component is different. Each component is in order when written in the middle-endian date format popular in the USA.

If you want to specify a date format explicitly, then you must write how this date would be represented using your format. For example, a little-endian date with a 24-hour time and an abbreviated day-of-the-week would be written as the string `"2006-1-2 (Mon) 15:04:05"`.

The package provides several standard formats. The most useful is `time.RFC3339`. This defines the long format from ISO 8601 format, which defines the international standard for unambiguous date formatting. The example at the start of this section uses the `time.Kitchen` standard, which defines a simple format for times, suitable for use in locales that use 12-hour time.

Parsing Dates from Strings

```
6    var t string
7    fmt.Printf("Enter a time\n")
8    fmt.Scanf("%s", &t)
9    parsed, err := time.Parse("03:04PM", t)
10   if err != nil {
11     parsed, err = time.Parse("15:04", t)
12   }
13   if err != nil {
14     fmt.Printf("Error: %s\n", err.Error())
15   } else {
16     fmt.Printf("Time in seconds since the Epoc: %d\
           n", parsed.Unix())
17   }
```

From: parseTime.go

The `Parse()` function is the inverse of the `Format()` method. It allows you to construct a `Time` structure from a string, with a specified format.

The format string is the first argument and is in the format discussed in the last section. The example at the start of this section tries parsing two times: first as a 12-hour time with an explicit AM or PM, and then as a 24-hour time. If neither of these works, then it gives up.

You'll notice, if you run this example, that the seconds since the epoc is always a large negative number. This is because the date component of the parsed time will be 0, putting the time about two millennia in the past.

If you want the time to be relative to today, then you need to explicitly set the date part.

Calculating Elapsed Time

```
 7   parsed, _ := time.Parse("2/1/2006", "15/6/1982")
 8   now := time.Now()
 9   parsedSeconds := parsed.Unix()
10   fmt.Printf("%d seconds difference\n", now.Unix()-
         parsedSeconds)
11   diff := now.Sub(parsed)
12   fmt.Printf("%s difference\n", diff.String())
```

From: diffTime.go

If you have two times in seconds or nanoseconds, then it's trivial to work out the difference between them. If they are in calendar format, then it's different.

The simplest way of calculating a time difference is to convert both times to UNIX times, and then do the calculation. UNIX time is always in UTC: on UNIX systems, the system clock is set to UTC (or GMT on older systems) and the user-visible time is calculated by adding an offset to this time. This means that changing the time zone of the system will not confuse things like file modification times. It's a good idea to adopt the same policy in your own code.

The example at the start of this section shows

two ways of comparing dates. The first converts both to nanoseconds and then does simple subtraction to compare them. The second uses the `Sub()` method on the `Time` structure, which returns a `Duration`. This encapsulates a time interval and can be converted to hours, minutes, seconds, nanoseconds, or a string representation containing all three.

Receiving Timer Events

```
6   time.AfterFunc(2000000000, func () {
7     fmt.Printf("Timer expired\n")
8   })
9   timer := time.NewTimer(3000000000)
0   time := <- timer.C
1   fmt.Printf("Current time: %d nanoseconds\n", time
        .UnixNano())
```

From: timer.go

We've already looked at explicitly spawning goroutines to generate timer events, but the time package also provides some convenience functions for doing this. The `Timer` structure waits for a fixed length of time, and then either sends a message along its channel, or calls a function, depending on how it was created.

Using timers is usually more efficient than spawning a new goroutine. They are implemented using a heap. A spawned goroutine sleeps for the interval until the next timer is due to run, and then fires all timers that have expired when it wakes up. This means that you only have one parallel goroutine running, no matter how many timers you use. Spawning a goroutine is quite cheap, but not spawning a goroutine is usually even cheaper.

It's not always quite so clear cut. The timer, as currently implemented, uses a mutex to protect the heap, which means that there is the possibility of contention if you are concurrently creating a lot of timers. In practice, however, it's always likely to be more efficient to use a timer than implement your own version.

If you create a timer with `NewTimer`, then it will send the current nanosecond time along the channel created as its `C` field when it expires. If you call `AfterFunc()` instead, then the channel will not be used. The function that you pass will be called in its own goroutine when the timer expires.

Timers do not make any real-time guarantees. The timer is guaranteed not to be triggered before the timeout expires, but it may be triggered any time after that, depending on the machine load, the accuracy of the available timers, the operating system's scheduler, and various other concerns.

12

Accessing Files and the Environment

If you're going to write any nontrivial Go code, eventually you will get to the point where you need to interact with things outside of your program. The most common mechanism for persistent storage on modern systems is the filesystem, and it's quite rare to see a program that doesn't need to read files, even if it isn't writing any.

If you want to write portable code, the filesystem is one of the more tricky areas that you have to deal with. Any modern operating system provides a file store, which is a mapping from filenames to sequences of bytes. Beyond that, the semantics can vary considerably.

Manipulating Paths

```go
package main
import "fmt"
import "path"
import "path/filepath"

func main() {
  components := []string{"a", "path", "..", "with",
      "relative", "elements"}
  path := path.Join(components...)
  fmt.Printf("Path: %s\n", path)
  decomposed := filepath.SplitList(path)
  for _, dir := range decomposed {
    fmt.Printf("%s%c", dir, filepath.Separator)
  }
  fmt.Printf("\n")
}
```

From: path.go

File paths are one of the most common causes of headaches when porting code. These days, you generally only have to worry about Windows and UNIX paths, which use backslash and slash characters as separators, respectively. This is a significant improvement. Systems like MacOS Classic and VMS used other separators, and supporting all of them was quite complex.

When constructing a file path, you need to be careful to always use the correct separator. The *filepath package* allows you to do this yourself, using the filepath.Separator or filepath.SeparatorString constants. These store the character or string representation of

the separator, respectively. It's a good idea
to use the string version, because you may
find that you eventually want to run your Go
code on a platform that uses a multicharacter
separator, such as ::, although no such platforms
are supported by the current implementation.

There are very few situations in which
constructing a path using string manipulation
is actually the right thing to do. In most cases,
you want to use the `Join()` and `SplitList()`
functions. These combine a slice of strings into
a single string with the correct path separators
and separate a string into its components,
respectively.

Note how the `Join()` function is called in the
example. This is an example of a *variadic
function*, like `Printf()`. Unlike C, variadic
functions in Go can be called either by an
explicit argument list or by a slice. The ...
suffix on the slice indicates that it should be
passed as the variadic argument set, rather than
as a single argument. This appears redundant
here, but it can be important. If the function
accepted variadic arguments of the empty
interface type, then the slice could be passed
either as the argument list or as the only
element in that list, and the ellipsis is required
to disambiguate these two cases.

Reading a File

```go
func main() {
  file, err := os.Open("fileRead.go")
  if err != nil{
    fmt.Printf("Error: %s\n", err.Error())
    return
  }
  buffer := make([]byte, 100)
  for n, e := file.Read(buffer) ; e == nil ; n, e
      = file.Read(buffer) {
    if n > 0 {
      os.Stdout.Write(buffer[0:n])
    }
  }
}
```

From: fileRead.go

The *os package* contains a `File` type that
encapsulates a file and allows you to access it.
As with C's stdio.h, it also defines three always-
extant instances of this type, one for each of the
three standard channels.

The example at the start of this section shows
a simple program that reads its source code
and prints it to the standard output. This uses
the `Open()` function, which always opens files
for reading. If you need to write to a file, then
you need to use the more general `OpenFile()`
function and specify the `os.O_RDWR` flag or
something similar.

At the lowest level, file I/O works via slices of
bytes. A file is a sequence of bytes. Any more
convenient interfaces must be built on top of this

abstraction.

Remember that slices are immutable objects that represent mutable data, so the `Read()` function cannot modify the extent of the slice. When this program prints its output, it needs to slice `buffer` to the length that `Read()` indicated that it returned, unless the program length happens to be an exact multiple of the slice size.

When you reach the end of a file, `Read()` will return an `EOF` error and a zero length. In this example, we assume that the only read error is caused by reaching the end of the file, but for more complex uses you might want more robust error handling.

Reading One Line at a Time

```
13   lineReader := bufio.NewReaderSize(file, 20)
14   for line, isPrefix, e := lineReader.ReadLine() ;
         e==nil ;
15     line, isPrefix, e = lineReader.ReadLine() {
16     fmt.Printf("%.3d: ", lineNumber)
17     lineNumber++
18     os.Stdout.Write(line)
19     if isPrefix {
20       for {
21         line, isPrefix, _ = lineReader.ReadLine()
22         os.Stdout.Write(line)
23         if !isPrefix { break }
24       }
25     }
26     fmt.Printf("\n")
27   }
```

From: lineRead.go

If you are reading a file containing binary data, then the techniques discussed in the last section are fine. If you are reading a text file, then you probably want to read one line at a time and then do some processing. The *bufio package* provides a reader that allows you to read a line at a time.

When you create a buffered reader with the `NewReaderSize()` function, it allocates an internal buffer. In this example, that buffer is 20 bytes long, which is enough for most, but not all, lines in this file. The reader will read into this buffer until it finds a line break, and then return a slice of the buffer.

Because the slice is backed by the buffer, you must be careful to copy the data, not just the slice, if you want it to persist between calls to `ReadLine()`. This function returns three values. As well as the slice and the error code, it also returns a flag indicating whether the slice represents a partial line.

The example at the start of this section prints the source code for the program with line numbers, so it needs to be able to differentiate between reading a single line and reading part of a line. If the `isPrefix` flag is set, then it knows that it is reading part of a line. Subsequent calls to `ReadLine()` will return more of the line. The `isPrefix` flag remains set until it returns the last segment in a line.

If you're using the line reader, then you will probably want a loop somewhat similar to the one shown in this example, with each iteration of the outer loop processing an entire line. It would be trivial to write a generic wrapper around this that builds a long array of bytes for the entire slice. This is not provided by default, because doing so means that feeding it a file with a single 1GB line would require you to read 1GB into memory. Although this interface is slightly harder to use, it has the advantage that it uses a deterministic amount of memory, making it much easier to reason about your code's performance, independently of the data that it might be accessing.

Determining if a File or Directory Exists

```go
6    fmt.Printf("Enter a file name\n")
7    var s string
8    fmt.Scanf("%s", &s)
9    fi, err := os.Stat(s)
10   if err != err {
11      fmt.Printf("%s does not exist!\n", s)
12      return
13   }
14   if fi.IsDir() {
15      fmt.Printf("%s is a directory\n", s)
16   }
17   mode := fi.Mode()
18   if mode & os.ModeSymlink == os.ModeSymlink {
19      fmt.Printf("%s is a symbolic link\n", s)
20   }
```

From: isFile.go

Quite often, you will find that you need to check whether a file exists before you try to use it. This is not so important when you are accessing individual files: you can typically open them with a combination of flags that fails if they don't exist. Even if a file does exist, it may not be usable. If it's a directory or a link, for example, then you may want to interact with it in a different way than if it is a regular file. For example, if the user tells your program to open a directory, then you may wish to recursively open every file in the directory, rather than opening the directory as if it were a file.

The example at the start of this section checks

whether a named file exists, and if it does then it also checks whether it is a directory or a symbolic link. This uses the Go `Stat()` function, which wraps the `stat()` system call and wraps the returned platform-dependent structure in a platform-independent Go structure.

In particular, you should note how we check whether a file is a symbolic link. The `Stat()` call will attempt to follow symbolic links. If it succeeds, then the returned structure will describe the file or directory at the end of the link, which won't itself be a symbolic link, so its mode won't have its symlink flag set. If, on the other hand, the file is a broken symlink, the returned structure will describe the link itself.

If you want to inspect a symbolic link directly, then you can use `Lstat()` instead. This is almost identical to `Stat()`, but it makes no attempt to follow links. As such, the result from this call will not let you tell whether the target of a link is a directory.

Checking Environment Variables

```go
6    var debugLevel int
7
8    func debugLog(level int, msg string, args ...
         interface{}) {
9      if debugLevel > level { fmt.Printf(msg, args
           ...) }
10   }
11
12   func main() {
13     debugLevel, _ = strconv.Atoi(os.Getenv("DEBUG")
           )
14     debugLog(3, "Starting\n")
15   }
```

From: envDebug.go

Environment variables provide a fairly simple mechanism for setting some state for a program before it runs. The environment is a set of key-value pairs, which can be set on the command line or in code. When a program starts, it typically inherits the environment from its parent process, with any modifications that process made explicitly.

Environment variables can be useful for tunable parameters. The example at the start of this section sets an integer value indicating the debug level based on the value of an environment variable. If this environment variable is not set, then the **Getenv()** call will return the empty string and **Atoi** will return 0, so the default debug level is zero. If you want a different default, then you would need to explicitly set it.

```
1  $ ./6.out
2  $ DEBUG=4 ./6.out
3  Starting
```

Output from: envDebug.go

The environment is stored as an array of strings in the **os.Envs** variable. The `Getenv()` function, on its first call, copies the environment variables into a map, so subsequent lookups only require a map lookup, rather than a linear search. It's still relatively expensive to do a map lookup and then parse a decimal string, though, so this program caches the result.

Whether you need to do this kind of caching depends on the format of the data and how often it's called. A debug logging function is expected to be called quite often, and should return quickly if it is not used. Looking up the environment variable and parsing the integer value for every call would be expensive. In other cases, this is not important because the code looking up the environment variable either wants to access the string directly, is called infrequently, or does something so expensive that it's not worth optimizing this small part of it.

13

Network Access

When C was created, computers were rare and expensive. It was still fairly common for a company to have a single computer. Now, a computer that isn't connected to a network is considered an oddity.

Being able to interact with the network is important for most programs. Go has a variety of packages in the standard library for network access, which is hardly surprising when you consider that Google is the language's main backer.

Connecting to Servers

```
6   func tryConnect(network, host string, port int)
        net.Conn {
7     p := strconv.Itoa(port)
8     addr := net.JoinHostPort(host, p)
9     c, e := net.Dial(network, addr)
10    if e == nil { return c }
11    return nil
12  }
```

From: connect.go

If you are used to high-level languages, then
you will find Go's basic network support quite
primitive. Go incorporates convenient high-level
wrappers for various protocols, but the socket-
style APIs are somewhat baroque.

The example at the start of this section shows
how to connect, given a host, a network, and
a port. The host can be any network address.
The network indicates the lower-layer protocol.
For example, "tcp" indicates a TCP connection,
running on either IPv4 or IPv6, while "udp6"
indicates a UDP connection running on top of
IPv6.

The Dial() function from the net package is
responsible for creating the connection. This
either returns an error or a valid connection.
This takes the address as a single string,
containing the host's address and port number,
so you must first combine these two values into a
single string using the JoinHostPort() function.

Before you can use this function, you must look

up a valid host address and the port number for
the service that you are using. This is something
that would be done automatically for you with
a high-level API, but must be done explicitly in
Go.

```
14  func connect(network, service, host string) net.
        Conn {
15    _, addrs, _ := net.LookupSRV(service, network,
          host)
16    for _, srv := range addrs {
17      c := tryConnect(network, srv.Target, int(srv.
            Port))
18      if c != nil {
19        return c
20      }
21    }
22    port, _ := net.LookupPort(network, service)
23    ips, _ := net.LookupHost(host)
24    for _, ip := range ips {
25      c := tryConnect(network, ip, port)
26      if c != nil {
27        return c
28      }
29    }
30    return nil
31  }
```

From: connect.go

Unfortunately, Go does not provide a single
interface encapsulating the various low-level
lookup methods. There are generally two ways
in which you can get a valid port number. One
is via a static lookup for the IANA-assigned
standard port, typically listed in the operating

system's /etc/services file. The other is via an
SRV record, specifying a nonstandard port for
this service.

Go provides a mechanism for performing both
kinds of lookup. The LookupSRV() function
returns a list of SRV entries. In the connect.go
example, we just check these in the order that
they are returned, ignoring their weight and
priority values.

If there is no SRV record for the specified
server, then you must fall back to static
lookup, using LookupPort(). You can then use
LookupHost() to find a set of network addresses
that correspond to the host name, independent
of the service. As with the set returned by
LookupSRV, this example tries each one in turn
until it finds one that works.

```
33   func main() {
34     c := connect("tcp", "http", "informit.com")
35     c.Write([]byte("GET / HTTP/1.1\r\nHost:
             informit.com\r\n\r\n"))
36     buffer := make([]byte, 1024)
37     c.Read(buffer)
38     fmt.Printf("%s", buffer)
39   }
```

From: connect.go

The returned connection has a few methods
that you can use for network communication. In
this example, we've used the generic connection
interface, which just provides methods for

reading and writing slices of bytes. Packet-
based connections, such as UDP, will return
something implementing the `PacketConn`
interface, supporting operations that allow
writing packets to specific addresses and reading
packets along with their associated address.

Distributing Go

```
package main
import "old/netchan"
import "fmt"

func main() {
  counter := 0
  ch := make(chan int, 1)
  server := netchan.NewExporter()
  server.Export("Counter", ch, netchan.Send)
  server.Export("foo", make(chan bool, 12),
      netchan.Send)
  err := server.ListenAndServe("tcp", "localhost
      :1234")
  if err != nil {
    fmt.Printf("Error: %s\n", err.Error())
    return
  }
  for {
    counter++
    ch <- counter
  }
}
```

From: chanserver.go

One of the big advantages of using channels to
communicate is that it makes the distinction

between threads and processes more blurred. If a goroutine communicates with the rest of the program entirely via channels that copy values, rather than passing pointers, then it does not need to be sharing memory with the rest of the program.

If a goroutine does not need to be sharing memory with the rest of the program, then you can trivially run it in another process. More importantly, you can run this process on a completely different computer. All of this is possible with only small modifications to the code.

The chanserver.go file shows a simple example, a counter that returns a new value every time it is queried. The setup uses the *netchan package* to export a channel via a TCP connection, but the remainder of the code is unchanged. It would be exactly the same if the channel communicated with a local goroutine.

Note: The netchan package is in old/ and will not be supported in the Go 1.0 release. A new version is due to be added sometime after Go 1.0. This example will probably not work in an unmodified form with the new netchan package, but the core idea of simply rerouting channel messages over the network should remain valid.

Exporting the channel for remote connections is very simple. The **Exporter** and **Importer** types

from the netchan package handle all of the hard
work. They wrap a network socket and a local
channel, transferring messages between them.

Preparing the exporter requires configuring the
two sides: the local channel and the network
interface. The `Export()` method provides the
local part. It associates a channel with a name,
and specifies the direction in which messages will
be sent. Here, we are declaring that the channel
should be published as Counter and that this
process will be using the channel for sending
data. You can call this method several times,
if you want to export multiple channels over the
same connection.

The `ListenAndServe()` method is the other
part. It listens for incoming connections on the
specified network address and connects remote
channels to the ones that it's advertised.

The client, in the chanclient.go example, is
similar. The `Importer` works in the same way,
but in reverse. First it connects to a remote
server, then it connects local channels to remote
channels, identified by name. The `Import()`
function in this example constructs the new
`Importer`, connected to the server. When you
run this program, the results might surprise you.

It appears that the counter is being increased
by two each time. What's really happening is
that every other message is being lost. This is
because the `Importer` buffers received messages.
The server sends one value which is read by

```go
package main
import "old/netchan"
import "fmt"

func main() {
  conn, err := netchan.Import("tcp", "localhost
    :1234")
  if err != nil {
    fmt.Printf("Error: %s\n", err.Error())
    return
  }
  ch := make(chan int)
  err = conn.Import("Counter", ch, netchan.Recv,
    1)
  if err != nil {
    fmt.Printf("Error: %s\n", err.Error())
    return
  }
  fmt.Printf("Counter: %d\n", <-ch)
}
```

From: chanclient.go

```
$ ./6.out
Counter: 1
$ ./6.out
Counter: 3
$ ./6.out
Counter: 5
```

Output from: chanclient.go

the client, and another which is buffered by the
client. The client then exits, and the contents of
its buffer are lost.

As Senator Stevens would tell you, Go programs are a series of tubes. The capacity of each tube is the size of its buffer. When you place a value into a channel, it is stored in this buffer. If the channel becomes unreferenced, then the garbage collector will free it, and will also free all values stored in the buffer. You can think of a channel like a tube that you push balls into. When it is full, you must remove a ball from the other end before you can put a new one in. If you throw the tube away, then you also throw away all of the balls still inside it.

Try extending this example so that it doesn't lose messages. The simplest way of doing this is to export two channels, one in each direction, and only send a counter value in response to an explicit request. Most of the time, you'll want bidirectional communication, so this isn't too much extra effort.

Serving Objects

```go
type Counter struct {
  count int
}
type Arg struct { Increment int }
type Result struct { Value int }
func (c *Counter) Value(in *Arg, out *Result)
    error {
  c.count += in.Increment
  out.Value = c.count
  return nil
}

func main() {
  server := rpc.NewServer()
  server.RegisterName("GoCounter", new(Counter))
  l, _ := net.Listen("tcp", ":1234")
  server.Accept(l)
}
```

From: server.go

The *net/rpc package* provides a generic
mechanism for implementing *Remote Procedure
Call (RPC)* functionality. This is split into
two parts: one that is responsible for the
programmer interface and another that is
responsible for the wire protocol.

The package allows you to perform RPC either
via a direct socket connection or over HTTP.
The *jsonrpc package* provides an implementation
of the wire protocol component for JSON-RPC.
This is primarily useful if you need to export
objects that non-Go code can call. JSON-RPC
is a language-agnostic RPC mechanism and is

fairly widely supported.

The example at the start of this section shows a very simple server. This exports a single method, as `GoCounter.Value()`, via the underlying RPC mechanism. By default, this uses the *gob* encoding, which is a Go-specific serialization for objects.

The `Value()` method on the `Counter` is automatically exported, because it takes two pointer arguments and returns an error code. The two arguments are used for the input and output parameters for the RPC, respectively. When a request is received, this will be called with the received arguments in the first arguments. It should then fill in values in the structure passed via the second argument and return `nil`, or an error condition if it failed.

The `Accept()` method called here will handle each connection in a new goroutine: If you connect to this example fast enough then you will see a race condition. It is a blocking call, so normally it would be called in a new goroutine, but in this example the server does nothing except serve the object so that is not necessary.

Calling Remote Procedures

```
5   type Arg struct { Increment int }
6   type Result struct { Value int }
7
8   func main() {
9     client, _ := rpc.Dial("tcp", ":1234")
10    var r Result
11    client.Call("GoCounter.Value", &Arg{1}, &r)
12    fmt.Printf("%d\n", r.Value)
13  }
```

From: client.go

An RPC server is about as useful as the first telephone. A second telephone, or in this case an RPC client, is required to make it useful. The client component uses a very similar interface. The input and output arguments must be marshaled in the same way, into a structure with one field per argument, passed by pointer.

The example at the start of this section contains all of the code required to connect to the server from the last example and call its exported method. The rpc.Dial() function creates a new RPC client, connected to the specified network address. This is the same address that we passed to the Listen() function in the server.

The Call() method performs the remote call. This marshals the argument into the correct format for transmission, calls the remote procedure with the name given in the first argument, and then extracts the results into the structure in the second argument.

14

Web Applications

It should come as no surprise that a language developed by a web giant should have a lot of standard library support for the Internet. The *textproto package*, for example, contains generic functionality for implementing protocols that work on a challenge-response basis, exchanging lines of text. These include SMTP, NNTP, HTTP, and so on.

Go is now usable in the Google App Engine, so it's not surprising that developing web applications is one of the main reasons to choose Go. In this chapter, we'll look at several of the features that allow you to integrate with the web.

Integrating with a Web Server

```go
type webCounter struct {
  count chan int
}
func NewCounter() *webCounter {
  counter := new(webCounter)
  counter.count = make(chan int, 1)
  go func() {
    for i:=1 ;; i++ { counter.count <- i }
  }()
  return counter
}
func (w *webCounter) ServeHTTP(r http.
    ResponseWriter, rq *http.Request) {
  if rq.URL.Path != "/" {
    r.WriteHeader(http.StatusNotFound)
    return
  }
  fmt.Fprintf(r, "You are visitor %d", <-w.count)
}
func main() {
  err := http.ListenAndServe(":8000", NewCounter
      ())
  if err != nil {
    fmt.Printf("Server failed: ", err.Error())
  }
}
```

From: webServer.go

The simplest way of serving web clients from
Go is to use the integrated web server in the
net/http package. This provides a stub web
server that delegates the handling of requests
to your code.

The example at the start of this section is about

the simplest dynamic web page possible. It returns a plain text string with a message and an integer that increments every call. Note that the `ResponseWriter` implements the `io.Writer` interface, so it can be used with the functions from the *fmt package* and other functions that produce output of this kind.

When you run this example, you just need to point your browser at `http://localhost:8000` and you will see the output. Every time the server receives a connection request, it will serve a simple (text only) page telling the user his hit number.

If you are already running a web server, but want to provide some dynamic components from Go, then you should take a look at the *fastcgi package.* This uses the same interface that the `webCounter` structure in this example implements, but associates it with a path in an existing server, rather than a port on a new server.

This example may appear more complicated than required, at first glance. Why are we using a channel to provide a stream of incrementing integers? Couldn't we just increment a field? We could, if we used an atomic increment from the *atomic package*, but this is a somewhat cleaner approach.

Every time a request is received, the `ServeHTTP()` method will be called *in a new goroutine.* A simple increment statement is not atomic, so if two requests were handled at the same time then one of the increments could get lost. For an example this simple, that doesn't really matter, but in anything more complex it might.

Spawning a new goroutine to provide the sequence is an example of the share memory by communicating pattern that we saw in Chapter 10, *Concurrency Design Patterns*. Using this, we don't have to worry about concurrency. Each response will get a new value, irrespective of whether they are sequential or concurrent.

Note that counter values are not lost here, unlike some earlier examples, because all of the goroutines are sharing the same channel. The channel is not being deallocated with some counter values still stored in it, until the server exits.

Connecting to Web Servers

```
10    client := &http.Client{}
11    client.CheckRedirect =
12      func(req *http.Request, via []*http.Request)
            error {
13      fmt.Fprintf(os.Stderr, "Redirect: %v\n", req.
            URL);
14      return nil
15    }
16    var url string
17    if len(os.Args) < 2 {
18      url = "http://golang.org"
19    } else {
20      url = os.Args[1]
21    }
22    page, err := client.Get(url)
23    if err != nil {
24      fmt.Fprintf(os.Stderr, "Error: %s\n", err.Error
            ())
25      return
26    }
27    io.Copy(os.Stdout, page.Body)
28    page.Body.Close()
```

From: wget.go

A typical web application or web service acts as
both a client and a server, collecting data from
other web services and providing it to clients,
who may be end users or other web services. The
client part in Go is even simpler than the server
side.

The `http.Client` structure provides a very
simple way of communicating with web servers.
You can either construct a request yourself—
using the same structure that was delivered to

the ServeHTTP() function in the last section—or
just specify a URL.

The example at the top of this section is a
very simple tool for fetching a specified web
page, or the Go home page if none is explicitly
given. It then writes the contents of the page
to the standard output. If the final page
was found after following some redirections,
it reports each redirection on the standard
error. For every redirection, the client calls its
CheckRedirect function, if one is set. This
allows you to set custom policies for handling
redirections, although this simple example just
logs a message.

Note in particular how the page is written to the
standard output. The Get() method will return
immediately when the server starts delivering
data; it won't wait until the entire resource
has been downloaded. This is particularly
useful if the URL points to something like a
CD or DVD disk image or a large movie. The
response contains a field that implements the
io.ReadCloser interface. You can read the data
from this as it arrives. In this example, we're
just using the io.Copy() function to write it
straight to the standard output.

Parsing HTML

```go
tokenizer := html.NewTokenizer(page.Body)
foundStart := false
for {
  ty := tokenizer.Next()
  if ty == html.ErrorToken { break }
  if ty != html.StartTagToken { continue }
  t := tokenizer.Token()
  if t.Data != "a" { continue }
  for _, attr := range t.Attr {
    if "href" == attr.Key {
      if !foundStart ||
        ((len(attr.Val) > 4) &&
        "http" == attr.Val[0:4] ){
        if ".." == attr.Val {
          foundStart = true
        }
        break
      }
      fmt.Printf("%s\n", attr.Val)
    }
  }
}
```

From: pkgList.go

Fetching a remote HTTP resource is usually only part of the problem. Interpreting the result is the other part. Parsing HTML is a common task for web applications, either interpreting HTML delivered from another server or validating HTML uploaded by clients.

The example at the start of this section uses the *exp/html package*, which contains an HTML5 parser, to read the package list from http://golang.org/pkg/ and try to find the package names. This is a fairly simple screen scraper. It assumes that every relative link after the link to the enclosing directory is the name of a package, and writes it out to the standard output. Because it relies on the structure of the page, this example may break at any point in the future if the structure of the package list page changes.

Note: This example uses a package from the exp hierarchy, which is not part of the standard Go 1.0 install. To run it, you will need to download the exp packages from the Go repository. If you are using the trunk version of Go, you probably have them installed already. Packages in the exp hierarchy are experimental and are intended to become standard parts of the Go library when they are finished. If you are using a Go release after 1.0 then you may find that the package is available without the exp/ prefix.

Unfortunately, the html package expects well-formed HTML as input, so it is not useful for validating user input. It is, however, useful for interpreting HTML from other sources. Most HTML5 provides better semantic markup than the Go package list and you can use this package to extract and transform parts of it easily.

The basic interface to the HTML5 tokenizer is the **Tokenizer** structure, which takes a reader and then provides a stream of tokens. Rather

Note: The html package is intended for parsing well-formed HTML 5. If you are parsing XML, then the *xml package* provides a very similar interface.

than constructing a new **Token** for every token in the input stream, we call the **Next()** method first. This returns the type of the next token, allowing us to skip character data and close tags. If we've found an open tag, then we ask it to construct a **Token** structure representing that tag.

You can use the same approach when importing HTML, for example from ad networks or other third-party sites, to only allow a white-listed set of tags, simply discarding any that are not in your white list.

Generating HTML

```
6   type webCounter struct {
7     count chan int
8     template *template.Template
9   }
10  func NewCounter() *webCounter {
11    counter := new(webCounter)
12    counter.count = make(chan int, 1)
13    go func() {
14      for i:=1 ;; i++ { counter.count <- i }
15    }()
16    counter.template, _ = template.ParseFiles("
        counter.html")
17    return counter
18  }
19  func (w *webCounter) ServeHTTP(r http.
      ResponseWriter, rq *http.Request) {
20    if rq.URL.Path != "/" {
21      r.WriteHeader(http.StatusNotFound)
22      return
23    }
24    w.template.Execute(r, struct{Counter int}{<-w.
        count})
25  }
```

From: htmlServer.go

We've looked at how to serve data over HTTP, but the name Hypertext Transfer Protocol implies that we probably want to be sending data in the Hypertext Markup Language, rather than plain text.

The *text/template package* provides a very flexible way of generating HTML, and other structured formats. It allows you to insert placeholders into documents and then replace

them with dynamic data. The example at the
start of this section uses the counter.html file as
the template. This is a simple HTML file that
contains a Counter placeholder that we want to
replace with the actual counter value.

```
1  <!doctype html>
2  <html>
3    <head>
4      <title>Go Web Counter</title>
5    </head>
6    <body>
7      <h1>A Simple Example</h1>
8      <p>You are visitor: {{.Counter}}</p>
9    </body>
10 </html>
```

From: counter.html

The template package uses some of the
techniques involving the *reflect package* that
we will look at in Chapter 15, *Interacting with
the Go Runtime*. To see how it works, we'll
start at the end, with the **Execute()** call in the
ServeHTTP() method. This applies the template,
writing the output to the writer given in the first
argument. The second argument is a structure
with one field for every value referenced in the
template. Here, we use an anonymous structure
with one field, **Counter**, which is the current
counter value. Executing the template replaces
the counter placeholder with this value.

The **Template** structure was constructed earlier.
This example uses the **ParseFiles()** function

to create and initialize a template using a file on the disk. It will then construct an internal map of where everything needs to be inserted, allowing it to be quickly executed.

The template package provides a very powerful language for inserting data into the template. In this example, we've only looked at the simplest case—a single field being inserted once—but it's worth looking at the rest of the language if you find that this isn't enough.

While powerful, the template language is not as flexible as something like PHP: it is not a complete programming language for generating HTML. This is intentional. This package serves as an abstraction layer between programmers and user interface designers. The interface designers just need to tell the back-end programmers what kind of data they need. They can then generate templates for displaying it, without encoding any of the application logic in the presentation layer.

You may prefer to use the *html/template package*, which is designed to be used with unsafe input. It assumes that the template is sanitized but that the arguments to it are not. In this example, we are generating the arguments to `Execute()`, so we don't need to worry. If we were taking user input then having something else sanitizing it automatically would be handy.

15

Interacting with the Go Runtime

One of the advantages of a dynamic language is that the internals of the implementation are exposed for your use. This lets you do various metaprogramming things that are much harder in static languages. The *go package* and its subpackages let you do very complex metaprogramming by transforming the abstract syntax tree of a Go program, but even without going that deep into the implementation there are lots of interesting things that you can do.

Finding the Type of a Variable

```
8    switch t.Kind() {
9      case reflect.Int, reflect.Uint,
10         reflect.Int8, reflect.Int16,
11         reflect.Int32, reflect.Int64,
12         reflect.Uint8, reflect.Uint16,
13         reflect.Uint32, reflect.Uint64,
14         reflect.Uintptr:
15         fmt.Printf("%v is some kind of integer\n",
                 v)
16      case reflect.Struct:
17         fmt.Printf("%#v is a structure\n", v)
18         r := reflect.TypeOf(struct{ io.Reader}{})
19         r = r.Field(0).Type
20         if t.Implements(r) {
21            fmt.Printf("%#v implements the io.Reader
                    interface\n", v)
22         }
23    }
```

From: type.go

The *reflect package* provides true reflection. Reflection is a superset of introspection, but some languages that just provide support for introspection claim to support reflection. Introspection allows you to inspect low-level properties of various elements in a program, reflection allows you to modify them as well.

The simplest use for the reflect package is simple type introspection, querying a variable to find out its type. There are two important structures in the reflect package that you can use for this. These are **Type** and **Value**. The former encapsulates a type, the latter a value. You can construct either from an existing value.

Go's reflection support is limited to values. You can't construct new types at run time, but you can construct new values and modify existing ones using the reflection APIs. That's usually enough, because constructing new types at run time has limited utility.

One of the slightly ugly parts of Go is that interfaces are not first-class values. This means that the only way of getting the type of an interface is indirectly. In the example at the start of this function, we get a **Type** structure for the **io.Reader** type by first getting one for an unnamed structure that has a field of this type, and then asking for the type of the field. It would be nice if we could just do something like:

```
type := reflect.TypeOf(io.Reader)
```

Unfortunately, in Go, only built-in functions can take types as arguments, and the reflection APIs are not built in. As an alternative, you might think about doing this:

```
var v io.Reader
type := reflect.TypeOf(v)
```

This also won't work, because it's the value that is passed to the function, not the variable. The value is **nil**, and so there is no way for the function to know that we meant **nil** interpreted as a **io.Reader**. The work around that we use is to create an anonymous structure like this:

```
type := reflect.TypeOf(struct{ io.Reader}{})
```

This passes an empty instance of a structure
that contains an `io.Reader` field. The `TypeOf()`
function can then get the structure type, and we
can then use its `Field()` method to get the type
of the structure.

For primitive types, we just need to inspect the
`Kind` field of the `Type`. If this corresponds to one
of the primitive types, no further introspection
is required: if something is an `int` then you
already know everything about its type. If it is
a structure, then you can inspect its fields, its
methods, what interfaces it implements, and so
on.

Note that, for simple cases (including the
example at the start of this section), a type
switch statement will achieve the same thing
with significantly less overhead.

Finalizing Structures

```go
5  type example struct {
6    Str string
7  }
8  func finalizer(e *example) {
9    fmt.Printf("Finalizing %s\n", e.Str)
10 }
11 func NewExample() *example {
12   e := new(example)
13   runtime.SetFinalizer(e, finalizer)
14   return e
15 }
16 func main() {
17   e := NewExample()
18   e.Str = "a structure"
19   e = NewExample()
20   runtime.GC()
21 }
```

From: finalize.go

Since Go is garbage collected, you don't
need to write destructors. Once an object is
destroyed, the objects that it references will
become unreachable and they will be collected
automatically. Sometimes, however, you will
create a structure that needs to do some explicit
cleanup when it is destroyed.

In a lot of garbage-collected languages, there
is explicit support at the language level for
finalizers — methods that run automatically
when an object is collected. Typically this takes
the form of a specially named method.

Go lacks such support at the language level,

for a good reason. Finalizers do not run deterministically, and so code that relies on them is usually wrong. They should only be used for *defensive programming*, in case the user of a structure forgets an explicit cleanup, not for things that must be run.

For example, the `File` structure in the *os package* registers a finalizer that closes the file descriptor. This means that you can forget to call `Close()` explicitly before allowing a `File` to be collected and you won't run out of file descriptors. This is safe, because if the finalizer does not run then the operating system will close the file descriptor when the program exits. If code is required to run, for example to ensure on-disk consistency, then a finalizer is the wrong solution. This caveat does not usually apply to **defer** statements, because they will always execute unless the process image is corrupted.

In Go, finalizers are not methods, they are just functions. This has the interesting effect that different instances of a structure can have different finalizers, and they can even be closures.

The example at the start of this section shows a more conventional use for finalizers, where one is registered for every instance of a new structure when it is created. Note that we need to call the `NewExample()` function twice in this example for it to work.[1] This is because there is still a

---

[1] This may change with future versions. In particular,

reference on the stack left over from the last call
to `NewExample()`.

This is a good example of why you should not
rely on finalizers. If you change the second call
to just set the value to `nil`, then intuitively you
can see that the object is no longer referenced,
but the finalizer may not be called. If the
variable is set to `nil`, then the compiler notices
that it is a dead store and simply removes
the assignment, so `e` is left pointing to the
old value. If you call `NewExample()`, then the
compiler knows that this has side effects so
won't (currently) optimize it away. This is
highly dependent on the implementation details
of the compiler. Whether the finalizer runs
depends on the implementation of the particular
implementation of the compiler that you use,
which should highlight how unreliable they are.

---

there is currently ongoing work on escape analysis in the
compiler, so that the compiler will be able to manually
manage memory for values when it can prove their
lifecycle.

Copying Arbitrary Types

```
5  func copyAny(inV, outV reflect.Value) {
6    t := inV.Type()
7    if t.Kind() != reflect.Struct {
8      outV.Set(inV)
9    } else {
10     for i:=0 ; i<t.NumField() ; i++ {
11       copyAny(inV.Field(i), outV.Field(i))
12     }
13   }
14 }
15 func duplicate(in interface{}) interface{} {
16   outV := reflect.Indirect(reflect.New(reflect.
        TypeOf(in)))
17   copyAny(reflect.ValueOf(in), outV)
18   return outV.Interface()
19 }
```

From: copy.go

Copying is a surprisingly complex concept in programming languages. Copying a simple structure is trivial, just create a new bit of memory that contains the same values as the original. This becomes more complex when the structure references other values. Should copying recursively copy all referenced structures, or should it alias them? It gets even more complex when you think about external resources. Should copying a structure that encapsulates a file copy the file, or just give you another view into the same file? What about a socket?

Because if this difficulty in definition, the reflect package does not provide a single function

for copying arbitrary types. The example at
the start of this section defines a simple copy
function using the reflect package. This is
semantically equivalent to simple assignment
in Go, although vastly less efficient. It walks
structures, using their reflected values, and
assigns each element in turn.

This example does not follow pointers, it just
copies their value. You could try extending
it to use the same techniques shown in the
`duplicate()` function to create new instances
of structures accessed by pointer and copy their
contents. Although this example is quite simple,
it shows most of the core functionality of the
reflect package: you can use it to get the type of
a value, construct a new instance of a type, and
set a value independent of its type.

Constructing Function Calls

```
26    z := big.NewInt(0)
27    z, isInt := z.SetString(s, 0)
28    if isInt {
29      stack = append(stack, z)
30    } else {
31      m, ok := findMethod(s, z)
32      if ok {
33        argc := m.Func.Type().NumIn()
34        last := len(stack)-1
35        argv := make([]reflect.Value, argc)
36        argv[0] = reflect.ValueOf(stack[last])
37        for i:=0 ; i<argc-1 ; i++ {
38          argv[i+1] =reflect.ValueOf(stack[last-i])
39        }
40        m.Func.Call(argv)
41      }
42    }
```

From: calc.go

The reflection interface allows you to fully use the power of a dynamic language. It is almost powerful enough to write a complete Go interpreter. The calc.go example is a simple stack-based calculator that uses the *big package* to implement arithmetic.

The first thing that you should notice about this example is that it does not contain a command parser. When you run it, you can enter commands like Add or Sub, and it will apply them to the top elements on the stack, yet there is nothing parsing these commands in the code.

```
1   123
2   [123]
3   456
4   [123 456]
5   Sub
6   [123 333]
7   Sub
8   [123 210]
9   90
10  [123 210 90]
11  Add
12  [123 210 300]
```

Output from: calc.go

The commands that the user enters are mapped
directly to methods. The `findMethod()` function
uses reflection to find a method with the
specified name and then this is called, again via
the reflection interface.

```
9    func findMethod(name string, value interface{}) (
        reflect.Method, bool) {
10     t := reflect.TypeOf(value)
11     for i:=0 ; i<t.NumMethod() ; i++ {
12       if m := t.Method(i); m.Name == name {
13         return m, true
14       }
15     }
16     return reflect.Method{}, false
17   }
```

From: calc.go

Calling C Functions

```
1  package arc4random
2  // #include <stdlib.h>
3  import "C"
4
5  func arc4random() uint32 {
6    return uint32(C.arc4random())
7  }
```

From: cgo.go

Go, at least in the form of the Gc compiler, has a built-in foreign function call interface for supporting the de-facto lingua franca of the UNIX world: C. The *C pseudo-package* and associated tool provide a way of calling C directly from Go. This is very easy to use, in terms of source, but building code that uses cgo is slightly more complicated.

A cgo source file imports the C pseudo-package, immediately after some optional comments that specify include files, linker flags, and so on. The cgo tool processes the source code and generates several files.

```
1  $ go tool cgo cgo.go
2  $ ls _obj/
3  _cgo_.o          _cgo_export.h    _cgo_main.c
4  _cgo_defun.c     _cgo_flags       cgo.cgo1.go
5  _cgo_export.c    _cgo_gotypes.go  cgo.cgo2.c
```

Output from: cgo

The _cgo_defun.c file contains the bridge
code and must be compiled with the Plan
9 C compiler (6c or similar, depending on
the architecture). The other C files must be
compiled with the system C compiler and the
.go file with the standard Go compiler.

Note: cgo is only officially supported when
building packages, not when building programs.
If you are using some C libraries, then you should
compile wrap them in a Go package and use that
from your program, rather than interleaving Go and
C throughout your code.

This process is quite involved, and it's better not
to do it yourself. If you are using the standard
go build system to build your package, which
we'll look at in Chapter 16, *Distributing Go
Code*, then it will automatically invoke cgo for
every .go file that imports the C package.

16

Distributing Go Code

After you've written some Go code, there is a good chance that you are going to want other people to be able to use it. Because Go is statically compiled, you can distribute binary packages just as you would distribute code written in C, or any other statically compiled language.

```
$ otool -L 6.out
6.out:
   /usr/lib/libSystem.B.dylib
```

Output from: otool

Programs compiled by Gc are statically linked, so you can just distribute the output from 6l without worrying about any other libraries. If you are distributing code—especially packages—

in source form, then Go provides a few helper utilities to make your life a bit easier.

Installing Third-Party Packages

```
0  $ go get github.com/dustin/gomemcached
1  $ go install github.com/dustin/gomemcached
2  $ ls ~/go/src/pkg/github.com/dustin/gomemcached/
3  README.markdown        client
4  gocache                mc_constants.go
5  mc_constants_test.go server
6  $ ls ~/go/pkg/darwin_amd64/github.com/dustin/
7  gomemcached.a
```

Go packages, like Go executables, can be distributed in binary format. As with binary executables, these are limited to one architecture and one platform, so it's not the recommended distribution mechanism.

The go command provides a very easy-to-use mechanism for installing Go packages from source. Typically, you will use it in two stages. The go get command will fetch the code from the remote repository. Go knows about several specific code locations, including Google Code and GitHub. For others, you can specify a URL with the revision control system name appended, such as example.com/my/project.hg to fetch from a mercurial repository. The go install command then builds and installs it.

The sources will be put in the src/pkg directory

in your Go installation and the compiled binary in the `pkg` directory, in a subdirectory corresponding to your architecture.

The URL at the start of this section is for a package providing a memcached implementation for Go. If you want to use this package, then you should specify the entire remote path in the import directive, like this:

```
import mc "github.com/dustin/gomemcached/
    client"
```

This allows multiple packages with the same name to coexist, as long as they have different URLs.

There are lots of other packages available beyond the standard library, although, as with any other language, the quality varies considerably. You can find a list of most of them on the Go dashboard: `http://godashboard.appspot.com/ package`

Creating Packages

```
package eg

// An example interface in a package
type Example interface {
  // Returns the name of this type
  Name() string
  // Unique identifier for the type
  id() uint32
}

// Creates a new value implementing
// the Example interface
func NewExample() Example {
  return new(concreteType)
}
```

From: pkg/src/eg/types.go

We've created lots of packages already in the examples. Or, more accurately, we've created one package—called main—a lot of times. If you look in the pkg directory in your Go installation, then you will find one .a file for each package that you have installed.

A .a file is an archive—a static library. It contains the output from the compiler. The Go compiler, unlike a C compiler, emits quite a lot of metadata in the resulting binary, including the set of exported functions and types.

Small packages, including a lot of the standard library packages, are compiled from single source files. Others may be compiled from more than one. If you are compiling multiple files into a

single package, then you must pass them to Gc
as a single invocation. This is required because
individual files in a package may have mutual
dependencies, which can only be resolved by
considering their source files in combination.

The eg example package shows this. It is a
trivial package containing two files. If you try
to compile either in isolation, then you will get
errors. The pkg/src/eg/concrete.go file refers to
an interface that is not defined in that file; the
pkg/src/eg/types.go file refers to a structure that
is defined elsewhere.

```
 1   package eg
 2
 3   type concreteType struct {}
 4   const (
 5     concreteTypeId uint32 = 0
 6   )
 7
 8   func (s concreteType) Name() string {
 9     return "Concrete type"
10   }
11   func (s concreteType) id() uint32 {
12     return concreteTypeId
13   }
14   func (s concreteType) isEqual(o Example) bool {
15     return concreteTypeId == o.id()
16   }
```

From: pkg/src/eg/concrete.go

Source files within the same package may refer
to each other's private variables and types.
There is no such thing as a file-local variable in

Go. Source files are just a convenience for the programmer; they do not have any significance to the language. Unlike C, there is no **extern** directive in Go, telling the compiler that a symbol that it can't see really does exist. The Go compiler must be able to find all symbols that it wants to refer to, either in source files or packages.

Most of the examples so far have been self contained, so we haven't spent much time looking at Go's visibility rules. Other languages have a set of keywords describing the visibility of various symbols. Go uses a simpler approach: anything that starts with a capital letter[1] is public, and so can be accessed from another package. Anything else is private, meaning that it may only be accessed from the same package.

To build the package, you need to use the **go build** and **go install** tools. The build step is actually optional: if you omit it then **go install** will run it implicitly. Before running either command, you need to make sure that Go can find your source files, and that subsequent compilations will be able to find the generated package. This is controlled through the **GOPATH** environment variable. This contains a list of paths that Go will use, in addition to the install location for the main Go environment.

Go packages must conform to the same layout

---

[1] As defined by the Unicode specification, including non-Latin uppercase letters like Θ.

as the main Go tree. The directory that you add
to the GOPATH should contain a src directory,
which should contain one subdirectory for each
package. When you run go install, it will create a
pkg directory if one doesn't already exist and
will install the package there. You can then
import it just as you would any other package.

```
1  $ export GOPATH='pwd'
2  $ ls
3  src
4  $ go build eg
5  $ go install eg
6  $ ls
7  pkg src
8  $ file pkg/darwin_amd64/eg.a
9  pkg/darwin_amd64/eg.a: current ar archive
```

Output from: gobuild

Documenting Your Code

```
0   $ go doc eg
1   PACKAGE
2
3   package eg
4   import "eg"
5
6   TYPES
7
8   type Example interface {
9       // Returns the name of this type
10      Name() string
11      // contains filtered or unexported methods
12  }
13  An example interface in a package
14
15  func NewExample() Example
16      Creates a new value implementing
17  the Example interface
```

Go does not have header files to help separate
interface and implementation. This separation
is imposed by the language, and anyone reading
the source can easily see which symbols will be
exported and which are kept private.

Having to read the source code for a package
to understand how it works is not ideal, and
shouldn't be encouraged. The go doc utility
reads all of the source files for a package,
extracts all comments that appear above public
declarations, and presents them to the user.

Persuading developers to write documentation
is one of the hardest tasks in programming, so

godoc is intended to be trivial to use. There is no special syntax for using it: it extracts any comment that appears above a declaration.

Hopefully, by the time you've read this far, you've looked at the package documentation on the Go web site. If so, then you've already seen the output from godoc. In fact, you've used the tool directly. When run with the -http flag, it not only generates HTML, it also runs as a web server publishing the documentation.

You can specify the -src flag to generate internal documentation. This is less useful because people using the internal interfaces are probably looking at the source files, but the output from godoc can be easier to navigate.

Staying Up to Date

```
0   $ go tool fix -diff trimStrings.go
1   diff trimStrings.go fixed/trimStrings.go
2   @@ -6,7 +6,7 @@
3     func main() {
4       str := "\tThis is a string \n"
5       str = strings.Trim(str, " \t\n\r")
6   -   words := strings.Split(str, " ", -1)
7   +   words := strings.Split(str, " ")
8       for _, word := range words {
9         fmt.Printf("%s\n", word)
10      }
11  $ go tool fix trimStrings.go
12  trimStrings.go: fixed stringssplit
```

The Go language and libraries are constantly evolving. It would be quite frustrating to have to keep rewriting a large Go application to prevent it from breaking with newer versions of the language. Fortunately, this is not required: the fix tool will do it for you.

Since I started writing this book, the `strings.Split()` function that I used in the trimStrings.go example in Chapter 6, *Manipulating Strings*, went from taking three arguments to taking two, so I needed to modify it. The example at the start of this section shows how I did it.

I never entirely trust automatic code rewriting tools, so I chose to run fix with the -diff option first. This shows the changes that it will make so that you can check them for sanity. This change looked sensible, so I ran the tool again and it modified the example.

If you run go tool fix -help then it will list all of the modifications that it can make. You may find that you don't want to make all of these changes and you can use the -r option to restrict it to a list of only some of them.

17

Debugging Go

In an ideal world, you would write Go code,
compile it, and then it would work perfectly the
first time. In fact, you'll probably find that this
is quite common. Go is designed so that there is
little ambiguity in the source code, eliminating a
lot of common bugs.

Go is still a relatively young language, so it
doesn't have quite the same level of debugging
support of more mature languages. People
have been writing buggy C and C++ code for
decades, so there are lots of tools available to
help them.

Using a Debugger

Go versions prior to 1.0 included a debugger
called ogle. This is named after a company
named something like Go ogle that has funded
a lot of the development of Go. This was not
ready in time for the 1.0 release, so it was

removed. Current versions of Go produce DWARF debugging metadata, the same format used by compilers for other languages. There are some Go packages for parsing this, so ogle may be resurrected in the future. Until then you can debug Go code with a recent version of the *GNU Debugger (GDB)*.

Unfortunately, Go is only supported by version 7.1 and later of gdb. This version is released under version 3 of the GNU General Public License and so is not shipped by default on Mac OS X or FreeBSD, only on GNU/Linux. If you are using another platform then you will have to download and compile it yourself.

Note: On OS X, debuggers (and any other programs that inspect another process's memory state) must be explicitly authorized. You can find instructions for configuring gdb here: http://sourceware.org/gdb/wiki/BuildingOnDarwin

---

To start gdb, just pass it the name of your compiled Go code. We'll take a look at a slightly modified version of the overflow.go example from Chapter 5, *Arrays and Slices*, which showed a runtime panic caused by attempting to access a value out of the permitted range in an array. The modified version, sliceOverflow.go, does the same thing but with a slice into the array, rather than the array itself, so that we can look at slices in the debugger.

When we run this, in or out of the debugger, we get a run-time panic. We can put a breakpoint on `runtime.panic` to catch all of these, but this specific one is an index-related panic, so we start by putting the breakpoint on `runtime.panicindex`. Don't worry about remembering this: it shows up on the stack trace generated on the crash.

```
$ gdb 6.out
(gdb) source ~/go/src/pkg/runtime/runtime-gdb.py
Loading Go Runtime support.
(gdb) break runtime.panicindex
Breakpoint 1 at 0xfe09: file go/src/pkg/runtime/
    runtime.c, line 80.
(gdb) run
Breakpoint 1, runtime.panicindex ()
    at go/src/pkg/runtime/runtime.c:80
80  runtime·panicindex(void)
(gdb) up
#1  0x000000000000209a in main.main ()
    at overflow.go:6
7       fmt.Printf("Element: %d %d\n", i, a[i])
(gdb) info locals
i = 1
slc =  []int = {0}
(gdb) p $len(slc)
$1 = 1
```

Output from: gdb

The debugger does not have native support for interpreting Go types; this is provided by some extensions written in Python and automatically interprets Go types for us. These appear in the debug metadata as typedefs of a format that the script can spot and interpret.

When we run the code in the debugger it stops where we put the breakpoint: on the function in the Go runtime that generates the panic. This isn't a very interesting thing to look at, so we go up to the stack frame that actually caused the panic and look at the local variables, with the info locals command.

There are three locals in this function: an index, an array, and a slice. Only two appear in the debugger, because the optimizer has already removed the array. From here, it's obvious what the problem is: the index we are using is 1, but the slice only has one element (at index 0), so this is out of range.

To make absolutely certain, we can check the length and capacity of the slice with the $len and $cap functions provided by the Python script.

The GNU debugger is very powerful. You can, for example, configure breakpoints to only trigger when a specific condition is met, or break when a specific region in memory is touched. A full description of all of these features is far beyond the scope of this book. Check the gdb manual for more details.

Misunderstanding Memory Ordering

```go
package main
import "fmt"

func main() {
  var s string
  var flag bool
  go func() {
    fmt.Scanf("%s", &s)
    flag = true
  }()
  for !flag {}
  fmt.Printf("%s\n", s)
}
```

From: orderingBug.go

The Go memory model makes it quite easy to write concurrent code that doesn't do quite what you expect. Consider the example at the start of this section. If you look quickly at this code, you might expect it to spawn a new goroutine that waits for user input and spin until this input is received. When the input is received, the spawned goroutine will set the flag and the main goroutine will continue.

In fact, I have no idea what will happen if you try to run this code. When I run it, it asks for input and then infinite loops. According to the Go specification, printing an empty string and then exiting without ever waiting would also be valid behavior.

This is because Go places very weak constraints on the observability of changes to memory between goroutines. The compiler is completely free to reorder the setting of `flag` to before the setting of `s` within the spawned goroutine. It is also free to completely eliminate the setting of `flag`, because it is a dead store within the scope of this goroutine.

This weak ordering requirement is quite irritating when you first start using Go, but it has two significant advantages. The first is that the Go compiler is free to be very aggressive about optimizing code, without having to do complex concurrency modeling. The more important benefit is that it strongly discourages you from writing code like this, which depends on subtle interactions between shared resources.

The fixedOrdering.go example shows an idiomatic Go version of the same program. This is shorter, doesn't do busy waiting (so doesn't waste CPU and battery power), and is much easier to reason about and debug.

```
5    s := make(chan *string)
6    go func() {
7      var buffer string
8      fmt.Scanf("%s", &buffer)
9      s <- &buffer
10   }()
11   fmt.Printf("%s\n", *(<-s))
```

From: fixedOrdering.go

The easiest way of avoiding this kind of bug
is simply to avoid sharing memory between
goroutines. In Go, this is easy because you can
always use channels to communicate. You can,
of course, pass pointers between goroutines via
channels. The fixed example does this, which
avoids the need to copy the data down the
channel, so the overhead is relatively small.

Spotting Concurrency Bugs

```
11    c.count += in.Increment
12    out.Value = c.count
13    return nil
```

From: server.go

The example above is a snippet from an earlier
example, and shows the most common silent
error in Go code. As a stand-alone function, this
is fine. Unfortunately, it is not thread-safe and it
is called from multiple goroutines.

The offending line is the increment statement.
This will compile to a load, add, store sequence.
If the goroutine is interrupted in the middle,
then two versions of this function could load the
same value, perform the addition, and then store
the result, losing one of the adds.

This is an example of a race condition and
is caused by violating the mutable-xor-
shared principle, as discussed in Chapter 10,
Concurrency Design Patterns. There are several

ways of fixing this. We looked at one in the section *Integrating with a Web Server* in Chapter 14, *Web Applications*, where the shared integer was replaced with a channel that produced a sequence of integers. Another solution is to replace the += with a call to `atomic.AddInt32()` or `atomic.AddInt64()`.

The latter solution is faster, but it requires you to make sure that you use atomic operations every time you modify the shared value. The former solution is simpler, because the value is then no longer shared and so it is very hard to create a race condition around it.

There are still some concurrent problems that can occur with channels. The most common is caused by the lack of guaranteed delivery. Channels are buffered, so just because a send operation has succeeded does not mean that the value has been delivered anywhere. We saw an example of that in the section *Distributing Go* in Chapter 13, *Network Access*. That example involved a channel being forwarded over a network, but the same principle applies elsewhere. If the receiving end of a channel loses its reference then any objects still in the channel buffer will be garbage collected.

If you need to make sure that values that you send are really received, then you need an extra layer of buffering. When you send a message, you store a copy of it until you receive an acknowledgment. If the acknowledgment is not received, then you need some error handling code.

The synchronous nature of Go channels also means that they are potentially prone to *deadlock*. If two goroutines are waiting for each other to send data down a channel then you have deadlock. This is the simplest case, but it's possible to have quite complex dependency graphs.

There are several ways to try to avoid this problem. The simplest is to arrange your communication into request-response hierarchies, so no goroutine can depend on data from a node closer to the root of the tree. This can be quite difficult to arrange, but hopefully most of your goroutines will be leaf nodes, which don't depend on any others to be able to send a response.

Restricting Behavior

```go
package example

type Public interface {
  Name() string
}

type Example struct {
  name string
}
func (e Example) Nme() string {
  return e.name
}

func NewExample() Example {
  return Example{"No Name"}
}
```

From: conformanceError.go

When you start debugging, you have a large set
of things that can possibly go wrong. Anything
that you can do to reduce the number of possible
things that can go wrong is helpful. This is
the main reason why Go encourages you to
use channels rather than shared memory for
communication: it dramatically reduces the
number of possible interactions, and therefore
the number of places for bugs to hide.

When you start debugging, it's always helpful
to make sure that the code is doing what you
think it is doing. Go doesn't provide a built-in
mechanism for assert statements, for two good
reasons: they are often used as a crutch to avoid

proper error handling, and their presence in test code can cause tests to be skipped.

Part of the aim of omitting assertions was to encourage Go developers to write proper error-handling code. In Go, it's usually quite obvious when you're skipping error handling, because you have function calls that return multiple values, some of which are ignored. The first thing to do is check that you are properly handling errors, even ones that you think are unlikely to occur.

Type-related errors in Go are relatively uncommon, but are still possible. The example at the start of this section shows a (contrived) simple interface and an implementation of this interface, with a bug. The bug is a typo in the `Name()` method: something very easy to do.

When you compile this, it reports no errors, but something later trying to assign the concrete implementation to the interface will break. If the assignment happens via the empty interface, for example by inserting the structure into a collection and then retrieving it, then it may not be caught until some time later.

The fixedConformanceError.go example shows two possible ways of making the compiler detect this for you.

The first is to simply make the function return an interface type. This is only really viable if callers will only want to access the type via methods exported through the interface. If this

```
14  func NewExample() Public {
15    return Example{"No Name"}
16  }
17  func NewExample2() Public {
18    e := Example{"No Name"}
19    e.(Public)
20    return e
21  }
```

From: fixedConformanceError.go

is acceptable, then you should also consider
making the concrete type private and only
exporting it via the interface.

```
1  $ 6g fixedConformanceError.go
2  fixedConformanceError.go:15: Example.Name is a
       field, not a method
3  fixedConformanceError.go:15: cannot use struct
       literal (type Example) as type Public in
       return argument:
4    Example does not implement Public (missing Name
       method)
5  fixedConformanceError.go:19: invalid type
       assertion: e.(Public) (non-interface type
       Example on left)
6  fixedConformanceError.go:20: Example.Name is a
       field, not a method
7  fixedConformanceError.go:20: cannot use e (type
       Example) as type Public in return argument:
8    Example does not implement Public (missing Name
       method)
```

Output from: fixedConformanceError.go

The other option is to add a *type assertion*. This

tells the compiler that you think that the type
that you have conforms to the specified interface.
The compiler checks this, and tells you that your
assumption is wrong. If the compiler can't check
the type requirement accurately, then it will
insert a run-time check.

It's also a good idea to use slices to enforce
range checking. The overflowError.go example
shows a simple error, where you accidentally
overwrite a range in an array with a subsequent
call.

```
4   func setRange(i, j int, slice []int)  {
5     for n:=0 ; i<j ; i++ {
6       slice[n] = i
7       n++
8     }
9   }
10
11  func main() {
12    var arr [100]int
13    setRange(20, 50, arr[20:])
14    setRange(50, 80, arr[:])
15    fmt.Printf("Array: %v\n", arr)
16  }
```

From: overflowError.go

This example is trivial, but it's fairly common
to see concurrent goroutines accessing parts
of an array like this. The fix is quite simple.
If you specify exact ranges in the slice, as in
fixedOverflowError.go, then the code will panic
if it tries to access part of the array beyond the

range specified with the slice.

```
11   func main() {
12     var arr [100]int
13     setRange(20, 50, arr[20:50])
14     setRange(50, 80, arr[0:19])
15     fmt.Printf("Array: %v\n", arr)
16   }
```

From: fixedOverflowError.go

It's worth using this facility whenever you are
tempted to pass a slice to a function. Restrict
the range to the part that you expect to be
modified, and you'll get a hard error, which is
easy to pinpoint and debug, if it goes over. If
the broken example had used two concurrent
goroutines, rather than two synchronous calls,
then it would have generated the expected
result some times, but not others, depending
on the order in which the two goroutines were
scheduled. This kind of bug is very hard to find
and fix.

Building Unit Tests

```go
1  package eg
2  import "testing"
3
4  func TestExample(t *testing.T) {
5    e := NewExample()
6      // Don't do this!
7    _ = e.(*concreteType)
8    if e.Name() != "Concrete type" {
9      t.Fail()
10   }
11   t.Errorf("This test is buggy")
12 }
```

From: eg/eg_test.go

Go includes a simple but powerful unit test framework. The eg_test.go file shows a simple set of unit tests for the package in the last chapter.

These are run by simply invoking the go test command with eg as the argument. This will build the package along with any files with names ending in _test.go, and then run any functions that start with Test and have the signature shown above.

The argument to testing functions is a pointer to a structure used for reporting failures. This test will unconditionally fail, so you can see what happens when a test fails.

The error message just before the failure tells you what went wrong; in this case it was our buggy test that always failed unconditionally.

```
1   $ go test eg
2   --- FAIL: TestExample (0.00 seconds)
3     eg_test.go:11: This test is buggy
4   FAIL
5   FAIL    eg  0.012s
```

Output from: gotest

If the previous test had failed, then we would
have no useful error. This is bad style, because it
makes finding the cause of the problem difficult.

This test contains another example of very bad
testing style. If the type assertion had failed,
then this test would have panicked. There is no
recover() call, so this would abort without later
tests being run. This is a problem if you want to
be able to get helpful error reports from users.

Well written unit tests can be very helpful
in preventing regressions, but they are not a
panacea. Make certain that you are testing the
correct thing. One project that I've worked
on requires unit tests, and they generally test
the exact behavior, rather than the high-level
semantics, so a large change involves modifying
a load of tests, completely defeating the point of
the tests.

Index

The Go Programming Language

PHRASEBOOK

ESSENTIAL CODE AND COMMANDS

David Chisnall

Safari
Books Online

FREE
Online Edition

Your purchase of *The Go Programming Language Phrasebook* includes access to a free online edition for 45 days through the **Safari Books Online** subscription service. Nearly every Addison-Wesley Professional book is available online through **Safari Books Online**, along with thousands of books and videos from publishers such as Cisco Press, Exam Cram, IBM Press, O'Reilly Media, Prentice Hall, Que, Sams, and VMware Press.

Safari Books Online is a digital library providing searchable, on-demand access to thousands of technology, digital media, and professional development books and videos from leading publishers. With one monthly or yearly subscription price, you get unlimited access to learning tools and information on topics including mobile app and software development, tips and tricks on using your favorite gadgets, networking, project management, graphic design, and much more.

Activate your FREE Online Edition at
informit.com/safarifree

STEP 1:   Enter the coupon code: BBYZKCB.

STEP 2:   New Safari users, complete the brief registration form.
           Safari subscribers, just log in.

If you have difficulty registering on Safari or accessing the online edition,
please e-mail customer-service@safaribooksonline.com